Suddenly... It's Spring!

To Erika,
Enjoy!
Mary Lovel

by Mary T. Lovel

Dedication

This book is dedicated to

All of my Editors:

Kathy, Shelley, Bud, Debbie, Lisa and Cynthia.

Thank you for all your help. Also to my husband, Clyde who made all of this happen.

ISBN# 978-1-4507-0684-151995_PC
First Edition
Printed in the USA

Published by Sherman Publishing, Sherman, Alaska
Email: mary_lovel@yahoo.com

Cover art photography and design by Bud Lovel
Editor - Kathy R. Jensen

Printed by AT Printing, Anchorage, Alaska

Acknowledgements

My thanks to all of my family for their encouragement and love.

Thank you to Bud and Cynthia Lovel for their love and support and for the photographs of "Moose in Wasilla".

Special thanks to Richard Long, Retired Alaska Railroad Conductor for his photographic contributions.

Table of Contents

A NOTE TO MY READERS I

FORWARD V

CHAPTER 1   MY DAD 1

CHAPTER 2   WHAT DO WE DO ALL DAY? 2

CHAPTER 3   A CHRISTMAS TO REMEMBER 5

CHAPTER 4   ALASKA HARVEST 10

CHAPTER 5   ILLUSIVE WOLVES 16

CHAPTER 6   SUDDENLY IT'S SPRING! 19

CHAPTER 7   FOREST FIRE SCARE 22

CHAPTER 8   BIRDS OF A FEATHER 27

CHAPTER 9   WINTER HARVEST 29

CHAPTER 10   A WILDERNESS
THANKSGIVING 32

CHAPTER 11   BROTHER BEAR 38

CHAPTER 12   DANGEROUS STRANGERS
AND LOVING NEIGHBORS 40

CHAPTER 13   LOVE AND LOSS, JOY AND
TRAGEDY 44

CHAPTER 14   FURRY BEST FRIENDS 48

CHAPTER 15   OFF TO WORSHIP 55

CHAPTER 16   EDUCATION AND STATE
GOVERNMENT 58

CHAPTER 17   CALIFORNIA HERE WE COME! 62

CHAPTER 18   BLESSED WITH CHILDREN,
                          GRANDCHILDREN AND OUR
                          FIRST GREAT GRANDCHILD!........ 66

CHAPTER 19   GOING BACK HOME TO
                          SHERMAN 69

CHAPTER 20   HOME AT LAST 72

CHAPTER 21   IT'S *ALL* AIRMAIL NOW! 77

CHAPTER 22   A NEW ERA...................................... 81

CHAPTER 23   MOM AND I HAVE OUR
                          BREAKS 85

CHAPTER 24   FRIENDS COME TO CALL 87

CHAPTER 25   WEDDING BELLS............................. 89

CHAPTER 26   DEVASTATING LOSS 94

CHAPTER 27 CLYDE'S DREAM COMES TRUE....... 97

CHAPTER 28   FREAK ACCIDENT 101

CHAPTER 29   ANDRE, THE FAMILY 'WATCH'
                          CAT 102

CHAPTER 30   STRANGE ACCIDENTS................... 104

EPILOG   109

APPENDIX A   114

GLOSSARY   137

PICTURES   140

A note to my readers

Shortly after Clyde and I were married in 1954, he said, "Honey, let's go to Alaska and homestead some land." I thought he was joking, of course, and I replied, "Are you crazy? Why would anyone want to go where it snows all the time and is cold and everything is frozen? I have no intention of living in an igloo!" That's all I knew about Alaska at the time. That's all most people knew about Alaska, then. And so we went on with our lives, working and raising our young family, although from time to time Clyde would bring up the subject of Alaska.

Sometime during those early years I read a book titled 'Go North Young Man' by Gordon Stoddard which changed my mind about Alaska, but by then I had managed to resist Clyde's yearning for nine years. I have been sorry ever since we arrived that I made Clyde miss out on nine years of living in this great land.

From the time we left our home in the lower 48 and drove to Alaska with our four little children I wrote long letters to the families and friends we left behind. I wrote faithfully, every day, of our long journey north pulling our 41 foot house trailer with a ¾ ton flatbed truck, and of the time we spent in Anchorage. I wrote about surviving the Big Earthquake of March 27th, 1964 and when we finally filed on our homestead at Sherman, Alaska. I kept everyone informed to the best of my ability. I even managed to take some good pictures to help tell our story to those who had never seen anything quite like Alaska before.

For years everyone I wrote those letters to nagged me to compile them into a book. I had no intention of doing that! There were far too many other things that needed doing to take on that particular project. Finally, after saving my letters and photographs for years, they boxed them all and sent them back to me with instructions to take some of the adventures I had written about and put them in a book. And so I did, finally. I

called it "Journey to a Dream", and was surprised and
pleased by how well it has sold. I was even more surprised
(and pleased!) by my readers' requests that I write a
sequel. People wanted to know more about life on the
homestead, and about what happened to our children:
how they grew up and where they are now. I hope this
book will answer some of those questions.

*The Lovel family: Mary and Clyde, Shelley, Debbie, Bud, and baby
Lisa, just before heading north to Alaska. Picture taken at Ethel
Lovel's house (Clyde's mother) in St. Louis, Missouri. Photo by:
Ethel Lovel (1963)*

Briefly, Clyde and I have four children: Michele
(Shelley for short) is the oldest; Clyde Jr., (known to
everyone as Bud) is eighteen months younger than
Shelley; next came Deborah, (Debbie) who is eighteen
months younger than Bud. Our youngest is Lisa, four
years younger than Debbie. In the first book, I described

how we started out for Alaska in 1963 when Lisa was only ten months old. Debbie was five, Bud was six and a half and Shelley was eight years old. We home schooled all four of them after moving to our homestead, but the three oldest got a start in school while living in Anchorage.

On the ALCAN headed to Alaska!. Clyde is standing on top of our 41 ft house trailer; Shelley, Bud and Debbie on top of the homemade camper shell. Photo by: Mary Lovel (May 1963)

We lived 14 months in Anchorage, before moving onto our homestead in September, 1964, after filing an open to entry claim with the Bureau of Land Management. Clyde stayed in Anchorage, and worked until he sold the house trailer so we would have money to live on, coming home nearly every weekend on the train to cut wood, bring food, and make sure we were doing okay. After six weeks, he was able to come home for the winter, and shipped up all the household goods, lumber and other things we needed on the freight. Meanwhile, he went back to work when the money ran out or when a job opened up. Sometimes he would be away from home for weeks at a time, depending on where the work was.

After two and a half years working in Anchorage and other areas, Clyde finally got hired to work for the Alaska Railroad, and was stationed (for the most part) at

Gold Creek, five miles from home. This was certainly better than having him working in Anchorage and only coming home on weekends!

The whole purpose in coming to Alaska was to homestead land and build a home for our family. Actually it was Clyde's dream, and I just came along. My first book has all that information in it. Also how the sign came to be painted on the front of our house, very visible from the railroad tracks. Our homestead is located 32 miles from the nearest road, which ends in Talkeetna. There is a stretch of 55 miles altogether of no road access and everyone living along this stretch depends upon the Alaska Railroad for everything - transportation, freight, even rescue in case of accidents. We are grateful to have the railroad. The Alaska Railroad has always been our lifeline. All of us off the road system depend upon the railroad for everything. We like to call it the "Railroad with a Heart."

I never knew that writing a book could change one's life so much. But it certainly has changed mine. It has been loads of fun, meeting new people all the time and getting to know new friends from all over the country. I highly recommend it to everyone if you have such a thought...Just try it!

Forward

The winter of 1970 - 1971 was especially hard on me. I had missed my sister Kathy's wedding because I couldn't leave at that time. Shortly after she and her new husband returned from their honeymoon our father passed away. I loved him very much and his passing was hard on me. I felt as if I had lost my childhood family, my brothers and sisters were all leading lives apart from me. We had always been so close and I was missing them more than ever.

Early winter 1970/71. By April we got another six feet of snow, bringing the snow pack almost up to the bottom of the upstairs window. Photo by: Lovel Family (December 1970)

It seemed to snow constantly, too. The windows on the first floor were completely covered. It was so deep the snow top actually reached the bottom sill of the upstairs windows. So it was dark all the time, even during those few short hours when the sun was up, we couldn't tell unless we went upstairs to look out what was left uncovered of the window opening. And, as often as not,

it was cloudy and snowing anyway. I not only felt trapped,
I was trapped in that tiny cabin with four small children.

I guess I must have developed a severe case of
"cabin fever". I'd heard about it of course, but had never
experienced it. As the dark winter months dragged on my
mood sagged lower and lower.

*Mid Winter 1970/71. Looking south east from near the back door. The two
lumps of snow on the left are a 1955 Willies Jeep and a 1928 'Thirty' Caterpillar
tractor. The outhouse is the lump in the middle. Here, there is just over a measured
eight feet of packed snow, and the conditions briefly allowed for snowmachine travel.
Photo by: Lovel Family (January 1971)*

Going out of the cabin meant following
snowshoe trails – the snow was too deep and soft to bear
our weight so we had to stay on the paths. Using the
snowmachines that winter usually meant breaking a trail
with snowshoes first. But even the paths were so soft that
winter we had to wear snowshoes whenever we left the
house. Walking was hard work; working was impossible.

The snow continued to fall steadily throughout
February and March, and by April it was ridiculous, and
so was I. We couldn't even do our spring wood cutting
because the snow never froze hard enough for us to walk
on, much less drag wood across. It just kept getting

deeper and deeper, and my mood went down deeper and deeper along with it. I reached the point where I could not sleep, and I could not keep from crying. Once the tears started I could not stop them. I was angry and depressed and I wanted out!

I called my mom and told her I needed to get out of the cold and snow and could I come to see her for a week or so? She jumped at the idea. My timing was right, too. The airlines were trying out a new marketing angle called 'triangle fares': basically a three way flight. Mom would buy the ticket down there and wire it to our airport in Anchorage which would count as the first leg of the triangle. The second leg would be from San Diego to Honolulu, and then from Honolulu back to Anchorage. All this was for the same price as a single round trip ticket. So I ran away from home. On April 26th I took the train to Anchorage – alone – took a cab from the depot to the airport, picked up my ticket, caught the 11:30 PM plane and arrived in San Diego in the afternoon the next day.

Running away from home was fun! I ran all the way to sunny, snow-free southern California where my whole family was waiting for me. I was so happy to be there. My mom and sister Beth were both at the airport to meet my plane and we had such a wonderful time. It was great to see all my brothers and sisters again. I was especially excited to meet my new brother-in-law Dave and baby nephew little David.

Later, when Mom and Beth and I were alone, I told them why I was so upset and nervous: Clyde wanted to sell the homestead and buy a boat of all things! He wanted to sail around the world! He wanted me to find out how much boats cost and if they looked large enough to live in. Dear God, he wanted to give up our hard-earned home, take what little money we could muster and toss it into a hole in the water! He'd lost his mind!

I was counting on Mom and Beth to help me but I had not reckoned on how they – and most people – actually saw my life. I had no idea they thought I was "deprived". They thought it was a fine idea to sell the place and move away from that "hard life" so far away. I kept explaining that I did not want to sell my home! They didn't worry about that so much as Clyde's plan to live on a boat; that was just appalling to them. I finally managed to convince them that I was very happy with my homestead and did not want any amount of money for it but didn't want to fight with my wonderful – if slightly confused – husband about it. They agreed to put their heads together and see if they could come up with some ideas.

Mom thought if we overpriced the place it probably would never sell. That was a comforting thought, so we tackled the next problem: diverting Clyde from boats. Perhaps we could get him interested in investing in some income property, rental units, a duplex or even a house where the rent would make the payments and he could always sell it for profit and buy another or borrow money on it or some such. Well, ideas flew hard and fast and meanwhile I got busy helping Mom wallpaper a room in her house. Beth had just bought her first home, and had many projects going that I could help her with. Painting the picket fence around the yard, dyeing her old couch, and polishing the cabinets may not sound like good therapy to you, but it was heavenly to me. Even better, Beth had just sold a house and made a good commission, so she bought a triangle ticket to Honolulu and then on from there to Anchorage before flying back to San Diego.

While I was in San Diego, we went to the Sea World, a wonderful place! And Mom took us to see the movie, "Fiddler on the Roof", which was great, and Beth and I went to see a real stage play - a musical comedy with real movie and TV stars acting in it, called "Guys and Dolls". The main character in the play was performed by John Saxon, who was better looking in person than on the screen. It was funny and enjoyable. It was the first live or professional play I'd ever attended.

Several times Beth or Mom took me down to the harbor in San Diego to look at and take pictures of boats that were for sale. We looked only at the sailing kind, not the motorized ones. They all looked so small, the cabin areas, I mean; I just knew that I could never stand to be so cramped up in one of them. And they were all so expensive! Boats and airplanes were just big holes in the water or air to pour money into in my opinion. I had a bad attitude.

I enjoyed visiting with my sister Kathy and my new baby nephew, a real cutie. My two younger brothers were just finishing up school for the year, but when they were home we had a wonderful time mostly catching up. Paul, the youngest, was finishing up high school and Bobby was in college. John (closest to me in age) was in Salt Lake City where he had a meat packing plant. So I didn't get to see him that trip, but I talked to him on the phone as much as I could.

Beth and I left for Hawaii on May 14th. We arrived in Honolulu at noon, and I fell in love with the place. It was the most beautiful and exotic place I'd ever been. From all I had heard about it, I didn't think I'd like it. But oh, that clear blue and green ocean, all those tropical flowers and everything was so fresh and lovely. We stayed for a week in a nice hotel that was only two blocks from the ocean in Waikiki. The Ala Moana Canal was just across the street. We caught the bus to go wherever we wanted for 50 cents each and swam in the ocean every day at the public beach in Waikiki. It was so warm, clear, and wonderful, with tiny waves, since there was a coral reef not too far offshore.

One day we went to the Polynesian Cultural Center to attend a luau, which is a Polynesian dinner. We saw the show in the evening and came back to our hotel by bus. What a marvelous experience! We went on a dinner cruise on a sixty foot boat with two decks. It was very bumpy and uncomfortable out in the ocean. We pulled into Honolulu harbor so we could eat without the food flying all over the boat. It was nice, though, even if bumpy. We explored the Rainbow Bazaar, the Ala Moana Shopping Center, and the International Market Place - all different, exotic, and lovely. We went to the Kodak Hula Show and really crammed our days as full as possible although we didn't see a fraction of what there was to see there. We never got to downtown Honolulu at all; the closest we got was in the harbor on the dinner cruise.

Our week in Hawaii was over far too soon. Beth and I caught the plane to Anchorage where we were met by Clyde and the kids. Bud and Debbie were scheduled to make their confirmations the next day, Sunday, at Holy Family Cathedral in downtown Anchorage. We spent that night in the motel nearby and all went to the confirmation ceremony which was lovely. We spent one more night in Anchorage so we could show Beth around town.

The snow had all melted in Anchorage by then, but as we went further north on the train, snow began to appear here and there in small piles. There was some still at home, but mostly all of it was gone. What a difference from when I left just a few weeks before. It was good to be back. I was no longer stricken with cabin fever nor was I depressed or unhappy.

At first it all looked barren: the trees were all grayish-brown, the grass dead, and mud was everywhere. This is spring in Alaska – but we call it breakup. There was plenty of sunshine as the days grew steadily longer and warmer, and then, suddenly it was spring. The grass was green; the leaves unfurled making the trees look fluffy, alive and green. All was right with the world and with me. I was more than ready for another busy summer.

We had a wonderful visit with Beth, and I went to Anchorage with her when it was time for her to fly back to her home in California. I saw her off at the airport, bought some seeds and plants for the garden and took the train back home once again. Oh, but it was so good to be back!!

No one bought our homestead, though we did have a few inquiries. I had finally left it in God's hands, as

I should have done to begin with, but somehow we forget to trust and try to force things to go the way we think they should be. I had many boat pictures to share with Clyde and I told him that I did not want to buy a boat, or go sailing around the world in one. They were all too small and expensive. I did, however, tell him he could buy a boat when he won at least a million dollars in a lottery - but not before!

***

Bud driving the Gravely Tractor up the path from the tracks. Mary, Debbie and Lisa catching a ride in the trailer. The Gravely was our workhorse for garden plowing, planting and hilling potatoes

Chapter 1   My Dad

My father passed away in California near the end of 1970, and there was no way I could go to his funeral. Clyde was working at Whittier at that time, and the kids were still too young to be left by themselves. My mother said she would rather I remembered Dad as he was when I was there the year before for the surprise family reunion.

Both my sisters and my brothers were there with Mom, helping her all they could. So I resigned myself to the fact that I would not be able to go. Instead I did the best I could to remember the great time we all had with Dad and Mom the year before, in 1969. There had been no problem then leaving the children since Clyde was working near home and was able to be there for lunch with the family and also every night, and the foreman at that time was a relief foreman and very nice and saw to it they were working right in the vicinity of our homestead all that week. It made everything easy and the family was safe.

My father is on the far left in back by Clyde. This photo was taken in summer '70

My brother John had sent tickets to me and my sister Beth and he arranged it with our sister Kathy to just make sure Mom and Dad would be home that day, and she was the only one of the family who knew we were coming. John was at the airport to meet our planes, mine from Alaska, and Beth's from Missouri. John had come from Utah. It was a wonderful week, seemed to give a new lease on life to our dad. But he was only 61 when he died and it was terrible for all of us.

***

Chapter 2   What Do We Do All Day?

People always asked me (and still do) just what we did out here on our Alaska homestead all day. With no running water or electricity, we had to haul our water from the creek in the summer and chop and haul ice in the winter when the creek froze over. We melted snow for dishes, baths and cleaning, and carried in firewood in order to keep both stoves going. We had a wood burning cook stove in the kitchen and a wood burning heating stove in the living room.

This is one of the first pictures we have of the homestead. This picture is taken five years earlier from the same spot as above. Photo by: Clyde Lovel (October 1964)

We started out with just two little rooms, with a flat roof, but even so, we managed. After we built the second story on the house in the 1970s, all four children slept upstairs. Early on we built a bedroom for Clyde and I on the north side of the house. We heated our bedroom with a little potbellied stove (that was probably used originally for heating old passenger train cars), which was great to have in the winter, when the temperatures dipped well below zero. Our living conditions were much better with all the extra room.

The only schooling available to our children was correspondence courses sent to us by the State of Alaska. This took up most of the day during the winter. I tried to keep them to some sort of schedule so that we could take weekends off. But studies were sometimes interrupted (not that the kids minded!), when people stopped in to get warm, or just to visit and have a cup of coffee. The track patrolman, the section foreman and crew from Gold Creek had little gas cars with canvas sides, and no heat. When the snow was too deep to come up the tracks on his gas car, the lineman used his snow machine.

Mary, Clyde, and Lisa (back turned to the camera) with Johnny "Teddy Bear", the Mackenzie River Husky we inherited with the homestead. This picture was water damaged, but it still captures the early look of the original cabin. You are looking north at the south side of the flat roofed two room cabin. Right about now you are probably saying, "They must have been crazy!". We were. Photo by: Shelley Lovel (November 1964)

And of course there were meals to cook, meat to cut up, wrap and store, (when we were fortunate enough to get a moose, or when the train hit one). Then there were dogs to feed, and rabbits. In the 1970s we kept rabbits that we raised for meat.

Since we had no TV we all were voracious readers. Every one of us had plenty to do at all times. In our "spare time", we sometimes worked on art or craft projects, whatever was of interest to each of us. Shelley and Debbie were quite good at art projects, Lisa liked drawing also. Bud had leather craft projects, a 20 mile trap line and various projects depending on the time of year. I liked sewing and making things on my old treadle model sewing machine. It was not a boring life, and it still isn't. Clyde has his woodcraft projects, and his sawmill to make lumber with, which keeps him busy and a workshop

Johnny Teddy Bear

where he can putter around to his heart's content. I write, and paint with oils or acrylics whenever the spirit moves me, and do plastic canvas and yarn projects.

We still read all the time, and whenever we go to Anchorage or Wasilla for supplies, we visit several favorite used book stores and stock up, so that we never run out of reading material. Of course sometimes the house seems to be overrun with books, and then we have to decide which books we can bear to part with (to make room for more, naturally!). Now that Clyde and I are alone, we have an old TV with a built in videotape player, but it sits in the closet and we seldom even think of it. Maybe once every two or three months we will get it out and play a movie for something different to do.

***

Chapter 3   A Christmas to Remember

T'was the wee early hours of Christmas morn,
We were snug in our beds all cozy and warm.
Stockings were hung near the chimney with care,
Tree was all trimmed with no branches left bare.
While out in the darkness there blew a fierce storm.
Wind drifting snow and nothing was warm.
All of a sudden a loud thump woke me up;
And a wee voice cried out: "Oh no!"

I jumped out of bed, flashlight in hand, and ran to the living room where I found Lisa huddled near the wood stove. I said, "Honey, what's wrong, what happened?" She replied, "I fell down the stairs, mama, and I think I hurt myself." I quickly lit a lamp and when I saw what she had done, my first reaction was to faint, but instead I tried to make light of it so as not to scare her. She was only eight, after all. She had fallen over the side of the stairs and landed on her bottom on the bullet loading device which was bolted to a shelf attached to the wall near the bottom of the stairs, and ripped a long jagged tear on the fatty part of her right buttock, deep and ugly and bleeding. I said, "Oh, honey, you cut yourself, but it will be okay. Just lie down on your tummy and let me clean it and I'll put on a band aid or something." I made her as comfortable as possible, and meanwhile Clyde was on the telephone calling the Air Rescue at Elmendorf Air Force Base near Anchorage, to see if they could send a helicopter out but they said the storm in Anchorage was

Bullet reloading device Lisa fell onto on Christmas morning. The metal projection on the right is what tore the deep gash.

so bad with whiteout conditions they couldn't even take anything out of the hangar.

Our nearest neighbor was John Lewis, the track patrolman, who lived at Curry, ten miles to the south. Clyde called him to find out what we could do, because it was obvious she would need stitches. Clyde sat by her while I phoned the nearest doctor at the hospital in Palmer to find out what we should do for her. The emergency room doctor said to keep her warm and dry and as comfortable as possible so that she would not go into shock, and to get her there within six hours. He said if it took any longer than that he would not be able to stitch up the wound, and it would have to heal without stitches, but would be more susceptible to infection and harder to heal. He said to keep the wound moist with mineral oil and covered.

Track Patrol Gas Car. This small two man vehicle is used to inspect the track ahead of trains. This picture is looking at the south border of our homestead property in the background.

Meanwhile John jumped on his snow machine and drove it up the railroad tracks the ten miles to our house. The drifts were too deep for the little gas car he usually drove.

When John got to our house he looked at the wound and turned pale, but kept his cool and teased Lisa about maybe not being able to wear a bikini for some time to come. He wanted to put her on a sled behind his snow machine and take her that way the 32 miles to Talkeetna, but I told him what the doctor had said about keeping her warm and dry. So John got on the phone and called the railroad dispatcher in Anchorage and explained what the trouble was and the dispatcher said not to worry, the snow plow was somewhere to the north of us and he would send them down to get us and take us to Talkeetna, where the station master there would take us to the hospital, 90 miles from Talkeetna. There were no doctors or nurses in Talkeetna. It was 5:00 AM, Merry Christmas to us all!

While waiting for the snowplow to get to our house, we got warm clothes and dressed Lisa and packed a small bag for her and myself, since I would be the one going with her. Clyde would stay home with our other three children. It would be the first Christmas we spent apart in our entire marriage, but we decided to celebrate Christmas when Lisa and I got back, so we would have two Christmases. That made Lisa happy. She had been sneaking down the stairs just to get her Christmas stocking, when she stepped on the hem of her night gown which tripped her and made her fall. She was remarkably brave through it all, with a minimum of crying or fussing. Seems she didn't feel any pain at the wound site unless she moved suddenly, and so she was content to lie on her tummy. I think it helped a lot that she was not able to see the wound, because of its location, and the lack of mirrors in the living room helped.

The snow plow arrived within the hour and four men cheerfully came up to the house with a stretcher. We carefully placed Lisa face down on this stretcher, securely wrapped in a snug sleeping bag. The crew of the snow plow were all happy because this meant they would get to go home for Christmas, which hadn't been the case before Lisa's accident. They all had families, and were very kind to Lisa and to me.

We wore snowshoes down to the railroad tracks with two of the men carrying Lisa on the stretcher, and climbed aboard the caboose attached to the back of the snowplow. It was very warm in there, with a coal fired stove burning at one end of the car. John Lewis followed behind on his snow machine as far as Curry to be with his wife and two little daughters there.

The snowplow cleared the railroad tracks before us all the way in to Talkeetna, 32 miles, where Skip Spencer, the Talkeetna station master, had shoveled his station wagon out of six foot drifts of snow, and was ready and waiting for us with the car all warmed up and ready to go. The men from the snowplow carried Lisa on the stretcher to the waiting car and put her in the back, which Skip had emptied out, and we took off right away. It was a harrowing 90 mile drive to Palmer as the road was not often plowed back then and it was dark and stormy all the way.

Along the way Skip told us about his wife and family, who we had never met. He and his wife had nine children and they lived in the tiny three room railroad section house in Talkeetna. Skip said we would be spending the rest of Christmas day and that night with his family and that there would be a train running the next day, so we could go home. He told Lisa she would have a lot of fun playing with his kids, and that he had a couple of little girls close to Lisa's age.

About 10:30 AM we finally pulled up to the hospital. The emergency room doctor said it was none too soon; if we were much later he would not have been able to stitch the wound. He took out this horrid looking scrub brush and began scrubbing away at the wound causing it to bleed more and I could not watch. Lisa seemed to be taking it all in stride. I suppose the numbing stuff the doctor sprayed on the cut desensitized it so she felt next to nothing. But I did, that was my baby bleeding there and so I had to leave the room before I passed out and made more trouble for everyone. The doctor was very swift, put about 52 stitches in her and said she would have a bad scar anyway, but if one had to be cut, there was not a better place. No veins or major arteries or anything like tendons, just fatty tissue. He gave her a tetanus shot and sent us on our way. She could now sit, but sort of on one side, not to put too much pressure on the stitches.

By this time it was daylight, and Skip drove the 90 miles back to Talkeetna. The road had been traveled by a few other hardy souls and the going was somewhat better. When we arrived at Skip's house, we met his wife and children. We were fed a sumptuous dinner with pies and all the usual trimmings, and entertained royally. Such a wonderful family! They had little gifts for both of us – people they had never even met, imagine! They made us both feel welcome and their kids played with Lisa and she was happy as could be. Somehow they made room for us to sleep there that night, and we were most comfortable. What a Christmas day that had been!

I called Clyde at home and told him we were safe and warm and well fed and missed them so very much but we would be home on the train the next day to celebrate Christmas once more. He said our other kids had not opened even one present, and were impatiently waiting for us. It was still snowing, lightly.

The day after Christmas Lisa and I boarded the northbound train for home and were met there about an hour later by everyone. They had all worked very hard to clear the path from the tracks to the house and it had even stopped snowing, at least for a little while. In spite of everything, it really was a merry Christmas for all of us and we were happy to be together once again.

Lisa healed well with no complications or infections. Nothing else happened of an emergency nature to any of our children, but we always knew if anything did happen, we could count on the Alaska Railroad.

To this day, Lisa still encounters the (now retired) train crew, who make a point of thanking her for helping them get home for Christmas. When she was a teenager, this was a source of mortification to her, but she now enjoys the attention.

***

Chapter 4   Alaska Harvest

At the end of summer 1971 our friend Doug Dunn came up from Anchorage on the train to hunt caribou. Now, we had never seen one down in the valley, (although Louis told us he had actually shot one down by the switch one year), but we had seen them only up on the top of the mountains behind our house, sometimes, when we were up there picking blueberries. It was a long way to go for berries, but we had not found any blueberries down in the valley and there were acres and acres of them up on the mountain at several different levels.

Summer, 1970. From left to right: Lisa holding a cinnabarb pie she made, Bud holding a Marten and Mink pelt from his trap line, Shelley, my sister Beth, Debbie, and Mary.

After much discussion, Clyde and Doug decided to go the next day, and Bud would go with them. Bud was eager to go. He was 14 by then, had his own gun, and was a very good shot.

At that time we had a machine called a Ranger. It was a track vehicle with wheels inside each track. It was steered by a braking system. It had two seats and running boards over each track with room for several people to sit on the running boards. It would go over logs and even through water, as long as it was not too deep, and was a real work horse of a machine.

Bud driving the Ranger, Clyde driving the 1928 Caterpillar 'Thirty' tractor.

We had already been up the mountain a week or so before and had picked gallons of blueberries and cut the trail out as best we could, but not all the way to the top. There were alders everywhere, thick and almost impossible to get through. But Clyde had marked the trail with bright pink surveyor's tape because the last time they were hunting up there they couldn't find the way down to where the trail was actually cut.

Clyde and Doug got on the seats and Bud on one of the running boards and they took off. When they got to the end of the trail, estimated to be about four miles from the house they got off with their packs and guns and made their way up the rest of the mountain, about another three miles all told. It was rough going for sure, but a lone caribou was waiting for them. Doug shot it and they made their way to where it had fallen, skinned and quartered it and packed all the meat back to the Ranger.

They fastened the meat firmly to the running boards and took off.

Part way down the mountain, Bud noticed a bear following them. It was a good size black bear, and of course Bud wanted to shoot it. But the men said no, they were too tired to skin out another animal. They shot over it, and it ran off in another direction.

Bud repairing the Ranger track. Equipment repair was a constant activity on the homestead. Improvisation until parts arrived from town was often needed. When Clyde was working away from home, Bud was often left to do man sized jobs by himself.

Later on, another black bear was following them, and Clyde put a bullet in the path in front of the bear, sending a shower of dirt and pebbles at the creature. It, too, ran away.

Before they were all the way down the mountain, a third bear, largest of them all was stalking them. Clyde stopped the Ranger, and the men all stood up and yelled and waved. Luckily for the bear, he too ran away. And so they got home safely with the meat intact.

The girls and I fixed dinner while the men hung the meat up in the shed with a light smoke on it to keep flies off. We had a lovely dinner of fresh caribou steak, and was it ever delicious! The men were exhausted; it had been a long day. The next day we wrapped and boxed the meat up for Doug to take home on the train. He left half the meat with us. It was still too warm to keep it, and we had no refrigeration at that time, except for a chest freezer in the basement at the section house at Gold Creek. I canned some of the meat, and we cut and wrapped and labeled the rest and sent it up to Gold Creek to the freezer there with Clyde when he went to work.

I had a pressure canner, and used either pint or quart jars to can meat and fish. I also had a Ball canning book which came with my canner, and it was a big help. Someone recently asked me for a recipe for canning meat or fish. I got all my information and recipes from my Ball canning book and nearly wore that book out, referring to it for everything I canned which over the years were hundreds and hundreds of jars of vegetables, meat, and fish.

Mary and Lisa with a head of cabbage, a turnip and some potatoes from the garden. In the background are about 300 quart jars of berries, vegetables and meat -Mary put up during the summer and fall harvest.

Already that summer the girls and I had canned 47 quarts of cranberry juice, some of which we would use for punch, and some for jelly. I put up 32 quarts of sauerkraut, from cabbages grown in our bountiful garden. We made jam from some of the blueberries, and canned still more pints of blueberries for future pies. I also had 14 quarts of beets canned and a few pints of carrots and two quarts of peas.

When Clyde's mom came to spend a summer with us, she liked to make cranberry dumplings with some of the juice. She made the best dumplings I have ever tasted, no matter whether with chicken or other meat, or with fruit or berries.

As far as recipes go, I put the raw meat, cut into chunks, in clean sterile jars, adding a half teaspoon salt to a pint, or one teaspoon to a quart. The canning book said to brown the meat first, but that was too much trouble for me and too time consuming, and messy and besides the only difference was the color of the meat when it was done pressure cooking in the jars. It was cooked for 90 minutes at 10 pounds pressure. It was the same for salmon.

I usually used only pints for fish. It was recommended to use half-pints, but with our large family of six - eight when my two little brothers were with us - half pints were not practical at all. I had great success canning as long as I could do it on the gas stove, not the wood stove. The woodstove was just too hard to regulate and the heat would have driven us out of the house! Nevertheless, it was time consuming as I had to watch the pressure gauge every minute so the pressure would not fluctuate and to adjust the heat accordingly.

We had carrots and turnips in the cellar and the remaining heads of cabbage were hanging by the roots in the shed. There was no room left in the cellar. We had already sold over a ton of potatoes, and there was at least that much in the cellar.

Every summer I made many jars of Rhubarb Jell-O jam, which was a favorite with the kids and easy to make. For five cups of finely chopped rhubarb, add three cups sugar, cook until rhubarb is soft, remove from heat and add 1 small package of red Jell-O, (strawberry, raspberry and cherry are good) stir until well dissolved and pour at once into hot sterilized jars, seal.

When we ran low on sugar, which seemed to be often during canning season, we canned plain rhubarb in quart jars. It tended to turn gray-green with time, but that was easy to remedy. We mainly used the canned rhubarb in Cinnabarb Pies, a wonderful recipe that I got from Alice Erickson, a neighbor in Gold Creek. Each quart of plain rhubarb made 2 pies. (The recipe for Cinnabarb Pies can be found in the Appendix.)

***

Chapter 5   Illusive Wolves

Early one January in the 1970's, some wolves killed a moose calf about a half mile north of our place. They had attacked it from behind, as wolves do, and crippled it by severing the Achilles tendons. The track patrolman found it, dead but still warm, as it had been dead only about an hour. He came back to the house and asked Clyde to come help him get it off the tracks. We got to keep all the good meat from it; it was just like veal and so tender.

We had a Chinook wind that winter, which is a warm wind from the north, which melted most of the snow, and left the remainder sticky and mushy. The next day we saw four women on skis out on the railroad tracks. They were three schoolteachers and a nurse who had taken the train from Anchorage to Hurricane, planning to ski from Hurricane to Curry. But the snow was so sticky and mushy they didn't get very far.

The crew from Hurricane section brought the women in their gas car, at least as far as Gold Creek, and they then skied the five miles from Gold Creek to our house. They were exhausted and overheated from struggling in the sticky snow still left on the tracks. We waved at them and they came up to the house and stayed for coffee and then decided to stay for lunch.

I cooked steaks from the moose calf and they raved over the flavor and how tender they were. I tried to convince at least one of them to stay and teach my kids for me, but they couldn't. They all had jobs in Anchorage and were just on the Christmas/New Year break. They were very nice women, all of them young and single. I really enjoyed visiting with them. They wound up going to Curry by gas car. I don't recall who took them, possibly the track patrolman at that time. We received very nice thank you letters saying how much they enjoyed the visit and everything; and they hoped to be able to come back for a weekend sometime in spring or summer They were all new to Alaska, this was their first winter.

After all these years, we still keep in touch with Cathy Donahue, one of the teachers. She lives in Anchorage and is now retired from teaching. Most Christmases she sends us a newsletter telling of her exciting travels to Spanish speaking countries. She taught Spanish in a middle school in Anchorage.

December 21 at 3:30 PM: Sunset. The sun does not come above the mountains for several weeks during the winter at the homestead. It does come above the horizon, but the mountains block it from hitting the homestead.

Back to the wolves - they were still around, but they didn't bother us or our dogs. But we feared for a cow moose and her two calves, even smaller than the one the wolves had already killed. Clyde and Bud saw them when they were running the trap line one weekend. Clyde saw one huge wolf across the river. It was almost black. He was afraid those wolves would keep after that cow until they got at least one of the calves.

Clyde and Bud set traps to try to catch one or more of the wolves, but they were too smart. They managed to get the bait out of all the traps without snapping any of them. They never did catch a wolf.

I was actually kind of glad, because the wolves were beautiful to watch, and never bothered us or our dogs. Sometimes we would hear them howling behind the woods in back of our cabin and the dogs would howl back. The chorus would go on and on, lonely sounding and kind of sad.

The weather turned very cold once again - our warm spell was over with lots of hard wind which made everything uncomfortable. It had snowed again, about three feet and the wind was piling up drifts all over the place making it hard for Clyde to drive the snow machine to work. From about mid November to mid January we don't see the sun at all, and even though we have around four hours of daylight, it's not very bright, especially if the day is cloudy. Then it usually warms up and snows more.

The winter of Lisa's accident dragged on and on. It seemed endless. We were housebound much of the time since it had been too cold to do much outdoors, and we were all heartily sick and tired of it. I longed for spring.

***

Chapter 6   Suddenly It's Spring!

After seemingly endless months of white, and cold came the mud and mess of breakup, which is the Alaskan term for spring. The first hint of spring growth was the rhubarb. It would literally poke it's head up through the snow as the snow melted. There would be a pause for a few days after the snow was mostly gone, and then suddenly, everything was green. We had a lawn, the trees were bright green and fluffy looking and the snow was gone except on the most distant mountains. Suddenly it was spring, and the whole summer lay before us, short but infinitely busy. Sometimes it rained a lot, sometimes it was too hot, but mostly it was just an Alaskan summer, with lots of daylight; a real break from winter.

The trains would soon run daily instead of once a

Rhubarb sprouts!

The rhubarb pokes its head out through the snow. The sprouts are bright red and very noticeable.

week, and we could again flag them down and go on a "Turnaround". That was what we 'locals' called it when we caught a northbound train and rode it to where the southbound train met, sometimes at Hurricane or Broad Pass, sometimes at Colorado. At that point, we got off and boarded the southbound train, and rode it back to our home. Meanwhile, when on either train, we could have lunch in the dining car, visit with neighbors doing the same thing, catch up on news, and make plans for further excursions, then get on with our busy summer. It was a great break in routine and a change of scenery as well. Our kids loved it and so did I. Especially when my best friend and nearest neighbor Nancy, got on at Gold Creek with her kids, to do the same. We talked fast and made plans for other outings and our kids enjoyed each other.

We had a message system going with the section foreman at Gold Creek, before Clyde got hired by the Alaska Railroad. Louis Hammons was the foreman and whenever Nancy would bring a note by the section house and Louis was coming our way to work, he would stop and deliver the message and I would send a reply back with him. We made plans that way for several years. It was a break from the daily routine of our lives, and gave us something different to look forward to. On days agreed upon by both Nancy and I, we would each, with Nancy's three kids and my four, start walking on the railroad tracks. Nancy and her kids would be walking south, while I and my kids would be walking north. We usually met in the middle, about 2 ½ miles. We would sprawl on a grassy bank and discuss whose house to go to, and then proceed, and spend the night, riding the train home the next day. We had so much enjoyment out of those visits; it became a regular ritual almost. Of course both Nancy and I carried guns, in case of bears, but we had no problems, most likely because the children always were singing or shouting or making noise of some kind. There were no paths or trails between Sherman and Gold Creek, and we were always careful to watch for traffic and trains on the tracks. These days it's illegal to walk on the railroad tracks at all, and certainly no snow machines or ATVs are allowed, either. But back in the '60's and '70's we were able to do so without problems. We were always careful to get a copy of the lineup from someone if we could, so we knew who was on the main line and at what times.

The railroad does not have lineups anymore, and the only surviving section house is at Hurricane. Both the Gold Creek section house and Curry House have been torn down. Most of the other sections are also gone. The machines are better, faster, more powerful, and a track patrolman is used in times of fire or flood. Everything is modernized and better, but there are some things we really miss. Ah, progress!!

In 1973 (if memory serves) Clyde went to Anchorage in the spring and took the foreman exam (known as 'writing the book') and passed it so he was promoted to certified relief foreman. This meant that he would be traveling to sections along the Alaska Railroad, working as a substitute for the regular foreman, generally when the foreman went on vacation, or if he was sick. This would only be for the summer. If he was lucky, his assignment would be right in our area so he would be able to get home as usual. The new temporary assignment was to start June 15, until freeze-up came, and then he would go back to Gold Creek.

***

Chapter 7   Forest Fire Scare

The weather was very dry, windy, warm and sunny. There were lots of bears around, and they were mean that year. I guess it was because there weren't enough salmon last fall for them since the creeks had all dried up, at least the mouths of the creeks. We read in the paper that bears were killing dogs tied up in Fairbanks and other places, which was unusual.

On May 27, a Wednesday morning, Clyde went to work as usual. As he, his co-worker, Bob and their boss were running south in the gas car at about Mile 253.5, they encountered a big black bear on the tracks, just ambling along. He finally got off the tracks and went meandering through the brush. They stopped the gas car and Clyde got out and shot it with the .44 magnum pistol (one shot). It was about 45 yards away.

Since they were supposed to be working (not hunting) the three of them loaded the bear on the gas car and brought it to Sherman. It weighed about 350 pounds.

It was at 9:30 AM when they arrived, and they loaded the bear in our trailer and hauled it up to the woodshed with the Ranger track vehicle. They all came in for coffee and left to work again, leaving the bear for Bud and me to skin out and gut. We planned to stretch the skin so we could scrape and dry it later.

This was a fat male bear, three or four years old. It took a lot of time because we had to skin the head and paws. The foreman dropped Clyde off at 3:00 PM, quitting time.

Meanwhile I had a call from a neighbor that the freight train had started a brush fire between Sherman and Curry, and another about two miles north of Talkeetna. So when they stopped at Sherman to let Clyde off, I told Clyde and his boss about the fire but they already knew about it. They had called in on the dispatch phone and were ordered to go up to Gold Creek, grab their backpacks for fire fighting and something to eat and get back pronto and patrol all the way to Talkeetna.

I threw together some sandwiches and a thermos of tea for Clyde. Looking out the window to the south, we saw the smoke from the fires as well as flames above the tree tops. It looked to be about 2 miles or less from the house. The wind was blowing straight at us! Clyde got on the phone and called the fire fighting patrol at Talkeetna and Anchorage and reported it as a forest fire. They said they would send a plane up right away with equipment if needed.

The smoke was getting thicker and blacker and it looked closer than ever. Clyde's boss came to get him and off they went to fight the fires. The kids and I kept watching and didn't see any planes, but pretty soon we could see the flames above the tree tops again.

We had been filling 55 gallon drums with water and hauling them up from the creek and trying to set up our feeble little water pump. The big hose for our big pump had not arrived as yet. I tried to call Curry or anywhere to find out the exact location of the fire and could not get anyone. All the telephone lines were busy. The wind was blowing harder and the valley was filled with smoke. We could see the flames over the tops of the trees, and it looked like the homestead was doomed for sure.

I had the kids go upstairs and pack a few of their clothes in their sleeping bags and I rolled Clyde's and my clothes up in our blankets.

We started evacuating. We piled food, clothes and bedding in the trailer and Bud drove it to the creek behind the Ranger and the girls and I found enough boxes to put the cat and the rabbits in. We drove everything down to the creek, as far as we could get the Ranger, and hoofed it from there, with as much of our household goods as we could carry.

We attached the dogs' chains to the back of the trailer and brought them down to the river with us. We wrapped up the guns and ammunition in towels, packed another trailer full of rabbits, guns, ammo, and other stuff and took the whole kit and caboodle down to the creek.

I kept trying to call someone but couldn't get through. By that time the smoke was so thick, we figured we had better get everything down to the sand bar on the river, which was about the only safe place - no trees close, and no brush. We carried everything through the woods, making many trips each. We set up camp with a tarp by the water's edge. The two youngest girls, Debbie and Lisa, had the responsibility of looking after the rabbits, so that none of them got out of their box.

Bud drove all the machinery into the creek, and what he couldn't get there we put in the middle of our plowed field - propane tanks, gas drums, snow machines, etc. We cooked our supper by the river over a camp fire and waited. From where we were, we couldn't see the flames, being lower down than our yard, and a large island of big trees down river from us blocked our view. But it was still smoky even though the wind died down a little, so we stayed put.

The kids were all rolled up in their sleeping bags ready to turn in for the night at 9:30 PM. Of course it was not dark, but because of the smoke a little darker than normal. Clyde finally came about then. He was black with smoke and soot and really tired after fighting fire for seven hours straight. Help did come; they dropped seven firefighters and planes flew spraying a red fire retardant and they contained the fire.

It had only burned about 200 acres, but some places where deadfalls were burning were still smoldering. Helicopters flew in and dropped 75 more men between 9 PM and 11 PM to get it out all the way. It was a full five miles from our house, too close for comfort, but not as close as we had thought. If I had been able to get any information we wouldn't have had to move out so quickly. Anyway, our first real fire drill went off smoothly and rapidly. All the animals survived the excitement and were none the worse for it. We moved the rabbits back home and the bedding and guns and covered everything else with a tarp as we were too tired to do any more that night - especially Clyde.

After dropping Clyde off at Sherman, the foreman and Bob had to clear off a rock slide in order to get to Gold Creek. The rock had fallen while they were fighting fires, but they had help from the Hurricane section crew. They had fought the fires too. Just before they got to Gold Creek, the Hurricane crew shot another black bear, about 10:30 PM. We got to bed around 11:00 PM that night.

During the night, half the mountain just north of us at Sherman, fell on the tracks. Next morning, Clyde walked up to the rockslide and he spent the day clearing that away along with the rest of the Gold Creek and Hurricane section crews. The same day, the tunnel up at Garner (above Denali Park) caved in so the northbound passenger train had to turn back to Anchorage. We had no idea how long it would take to fix the tunnel, or when the passenger trains would be running all the way again. The tourist season really started off with a bang that year!

After the scare with the forest fire, we decided to buy PVC pipe to bring water to the house. We ordered 1500 feet of it so we could reach way up the creek where the water still ran in the summer. The creek is above the house that far back, so once we got the water running it would gravity flow by itself.

The day of the forest fire was a pretty scary experience. We thought as soon as the pipe came we would be a bit safer here. Even if the creek dried up all the way to the canyon behind, that much pipe would reach all the way to the Susitna River, at least, and allow us to pump water from there.

It was time to plant the garden once more and also to clear more fire break around the house. The next morning, when Clyde got up to build the fire in the wood cook stove in the kitchen, he happened to glance out the back window, only to see a large grizzly standing at the edge of the back porch. This particular bear had a reddish tinge to his coat, and was probably a four to five year old. Not huge, but not small, either. Clyde kicked the door to make noise, and the bear promptly turned and ran off. Clyde shouted at him as well, which woke up the dogs, and then they barked!

Both of us watched carefully all the rest of that day and carried the gun wherever we went in our large yard, but luckily for the bear (and for us!) he did not come back. Later that day we ran the generator to charge the batteries and usually when there was any sort of noise like that, nothing came around.

***

Fall, 1966. Harvesting Salmon from the mouth of the creek. From left to right: Debbie, Clyde, Lisa, Shelley, Bud. The salmon here are Chum and Pinks, or Dogs and Humpies as they are sometimes called.

Chapter 8   Birds of a Feather

By the end of that June, 1973 we had the PVC pipe and then had running water 24 hours a day, gravity flow. Just had to start it with the gasoline pump and once it was running, shut off the pump and the water just kept running. It was wonderful. Until freeze up, then the pipe would stop running until the next spring thaw.

It was so smoky that we wondered where the fires were. The smoke literally blocked out the mountains as if in a fog, and our eyes burned day and night. We had this before, every hot, dry summer. We attempted to mend the hole in the swimming pool and fill it with water, mostly for fire protection, also use it to water the garden. And if we had more hot dry days we could even swim in it. It was four feet deep and held nearly 400 gallons of water, when it was free of holes.

When next we caught the train to go to Anchorage for supplies, one of our distant neighbors was also on the train. We caught up on all the news from up and down the tracks whenever we took the train. Usually there were at least two or three of our neighbors and friends on as well. That trip Janet told us of a funny thing that happened to them. They raised chickens and had a large pen and chicken house. They began missing chickens, and could not find out how until one day Sam, Janet's husband, saw an owl fly off with one of the chickens in tow. The chicken yard was too large to put a cover over it, and they were trying to figure out just what to do to prevent any more losses. Owls are protected, and Sam didn't want to hurt one. But Sam went in to the chicken house to feed them one morning, and there, right in the midst of all the chickens, sat the owl on the roost. It was contented and happy looking, surrounded by all its' future meals, and the chickens did not seem bothered by this strange looking large 'chicken' perched amongst them.

While Sam was just standing there, contemplating his choices, the owl stirred, looking as if he was getting hungry. Sam quickly picked up a 2X4 chunk of wood and whapped the owl on the side of the head. The owl fell off the perch and Sam reached down to pick it up, noticing that it was unconscious. Sam was afraid he had killed the owl, but ascertained that it was still breathing. Wrapping it up in a towel he went inside with it wrapped securely, and called the bird rescue people. He didn't want to tell them he had hit the bird, so he fabricated a tale, and told them he had found it beside the road, and someone must have hit it a glancing blow with a car or something. The rescue people told Sam to bring the owl in and they would see if they could make it well again. Sam brought it in and after a few days, the owl was well enough to set free. I guess that owl learned its lesson, because it never came back. When Janet told me this tale, I could just picture this smart aleck owl snuggling down with all the juicy chickens, smug and warm and well-fed.

***

Summer 1970. We had a lot of visitors that summer; it was wonderful! From Left to right: Debbie, Beth, Lisa, Shelley, Beth's friend Ed Hamilton, and Mary. When ever we went more than a few feet from the house we always carried a gun large enough to put down a bear. The rifle is a 30-06.

Chapter 9   Winter Harvest

Another busy summer was over, much too soon, actually, and it was time once again to start school. The kids' books and supplies were shipped from the Correspondence School at the State of Alaska Department of Education in Juneau. The passenger train had dropped the boxes off just two days before, and since we could not put it off any longer, we got started. No more excuses.

The garden was empty; the cellar was full, the canning all done, and the pantry shelves groaning with canned vegetables. It was snowing out, and the woodshed was full of firewood. Bears were all hibernating (we hoped.) The only thing we lacked was a moose.

Moose season was still several weeks off, but we knew where two prime bulls were hanging out, and were trying to keep track of them until November 1st, when the second season started. We no longer have a second season, but it was nice back then, because at least it was cold enough by November to keep meat hanging in the shed.

Then whenever we needed meat, we would bring in a leg or quarter, hang it up in the kitchen over a wash tub to thaw enough to cut into useable size pieces, steaks, roasts, stew meat. We would then package the cuts and mark them as to what cut of meat they were. We kept the meat stored in an old broken down wringer-washer.

In the winters, we did our laundry at the Gold Creek section house, where we kept our washing machine in the basement. If we couldn't get up to Gold Creek we would send it with Clyde, if he was working near town. One way or another we managed.

Clyde and Bud did all the woodcutting and the girls and I helped haul and stack the wood in the woodshed. In the spring when the snow was frozen hard as a brick (usually in late March or early April) we would have a three day marathon wood cutting and hauling session. When the snow is frozen hard, and you can walk anywhere on top without sinking in, it is easy to work in those conditions.

Winter wood hauling crew. Shelley, Bud, Debbie and Lisa on the 1967 Polaris Mustang. We used dog teams for several years before we got this snowmachine in 1968. We kept one of our best huskies, Copper, around to pull the snowmachine back home in the event it broke down.

Before we started out, the girls and I would make up a huge picnic, enough to last several days, usually of fried chicken, potato salad, cookies and punch and pack it all in a covered basket, go out to the wood cutting site with it. Then we would dig a small hole in the snow, build a camp-fire, which would sink and sink as it burned making a big deep hole. We would then cut steps down into the hole, and when it was time, we all had a picnic lunch.

Meanwhile, the wood piled up and the girls and I would get busy hauling and stacking. One group of two girls would hitch the sled to the Polaris Mustang snow machine we had then, and haul the sled load of wood to the house. The other group of two would fill a sled while the first two were gone, and then hitch it to the snow machine when they got back. As long as the snow held hard, we worked, each day, until it got to the point where we would sink in, and then we would quit, take what was left of our picnic and go home.

This usually only went on for three days if we were lucky. That amount of time sometimes was enough to fill the woodshed for the next winter. We all enjoyed it as a fun time.

Copper and Lassie were the only dogs we had left at that time and Lassie was half collie and half Siberian husky, but had never been any good at pulling a sled. Her feet were too small and she would develop enormous ice balls between her toes. She was, however, great at having puppies, and a good watch dog and pet. Copper was really getting too old to work hard. So they just ran loose

He was a big beautiful white Siberian husky, and had spent most of his adult life working faithfully whenever he was called upon to do so. He earned his retirement. And Lassie just enjoyed life.

***

Copper when he was about five years old, getting some spring exercise.

Lassie was a beautiful dog, but was not trained for sled pulling.

Chapter 10 A Wilderness Thanksgiving

By Thanksgiving we had another snow machine. Three weeks before then we had asked Bill Thompson, a crusty old bachelor who lived at Gold Creek, to come down and have dinner with us. He said he would let us know, he wasn't sure if he would still be up in Gold Creek then or not. He was getting ready to retire from the Alaska Railroad. So the day before Thanksgiving he told Clyde he couldn't come because everybody from Gold Creek got on the train Wednesday night and left. He couldn't get into the section house, to use the phone to find out where the trains were.

Well, Thursday morning Clyde called Curry and found out there were no trains until evening, so all four kids got on the two snow machines and went up the tracks to Gold Creek and bullied poor old Bill into coming down for dinner. That poor guy, all alone up there with just a little pot of beans cooking on the stove and nothing else!

He got on his snow machine and came on down with two of the kids on one of our machines in front of him and the other two on our other machine behind him. They got here about 11:30 AM and we served dinner around 1:30 or 2:00.

And what a Thanksgiving feast it was - we had ham, sweet potatoes, mashed potatoes, canned corn on the cob, hot yeast rolls, lime Jell-o salad with cream cheese, pineapple, carrot shreds and raisins in it and of course one of our two quarts of good garden peas, and were they ever good! We saved the other quart for Christmas dinner to go with the turkey. We had the traditional Thanksgiving dessert - pumpkin pie and whipped cream.

The whole dinner was very fattening and pretty good if I do say so and, I'm sure Bill enjoyed himself even though he claimed to be antisocial. Clyde said he hadn't seen Bill eat so much in a long time. I guess living alone he didn't bother cooking but just what he had to. He finally left for Gold Creek at about 4 o'clock. By then it was extremely cold at 10 degrees below zero, so he had a cold five mile drive home!

The kids all enjoyed old Bill - he always came up to the house whenever Louis, who used to be the section foreman at Gold Creek stopped to see if we were okay, and Bill's favorite of all the kids was Lisa, his "little blonde sweetheart". But he liked all the rest of them as well, including my two youngest brothers, Bobby and Paul, when they were here.

We were expecting my little brother Paul to come visit from California. He arrived December 9th and was staying until January 6th. We were so happy to have him back, even for so short a time. He was 16, which made a grand total of four teen-agers in the house at once. God help us all!! He was quite a handsome kid, a full six foot three inches and 245 pounds of muscle – my "baby" brother indeed!! He is seven months younger than our oldest daughter, Shelley.

We had an especially good Christmas that year because John Lewis called and told Clyde that the freight had hit a moose a couple of miles above Gold Creek. Clyde, Bud and Paul left on both snow machines and sleds and went up there. It was a cow, had a broken back and caved in ribs, which had punctured the heart and lungs badly, but the poor thing was still alive somehow. Clyde shot the cow and they quartered it and brought home all the meat, except for a front shoulder which they left with Bill. We use the bruised parts for dog meat and we humans had fresh good meat again.

Paul spent Christmas with us, and for Christmas dinner we had turkey, with stuffing, gravy, mashed potatoes because that was everyone's favorite, the other quart of peas, candied yams and blueberry pie with whipped cream as well as olives, pickles, cranberry sauce, celery stalks stuffed with cream cheese, and hot rolls.

Doug and Marie Dunn and their two girls, Julia and Beverly, came up from Anchorage Christmas day on the train, in time to share Christmas dinner. We enjoyed having them here so much. We had a lot of fun. The next day was Sunday and they went back to Anchorage on the train, but not empty handed. We sent a moose hindquarter with them.

That Sunday night I cut up the rest of the meat from the other hind leg, wrapped it all up and labeled it. I guessed that I got about 90 pounds of useable meat from just that one leg. The front leg was hung in the shed, and the one useable rib cage, so we were set for meat for awhile. We were beginning to think we would have to go on welfare because meat prices were so high. It was getting to be an awful strain financially, to keep us in meat.

Mary cutting up a moose leg. Clyde is behind, in the shadows.

Doug Dunn was home on a 30 day leave from Oklahoma, where the Air Force had sent him, and he was getting out of the service about the end of February. When Paul came, I gave Marie a check and she bought us some meat on the base, 55 or 60 pounds of it, much cheaper than at any store. She bought roasts, burger, our Christmas turkey, two big hams, cube steaks, ribs.

Then I bought twelve live hens from Milton Lichtenwalner, a farmer in Talkeetna. We had bought fresh eggs and milk from him a few times. He sold us those old hens for $1 each.

I had called Milton and asked if he sold any of his chickens for eating and he said he had about a hundred of them to get rid of and was selling them for 75 cents a pound dressed out and for $1 each live. They each weighed about 3 ½ pounds dressed out.

He said it would cost me $5.55 minimum express rate for 100 pounds of hens or less, live, plus $1.25 railroad handling charge and we could get about 22 hens for that amount, but I didn't see how we could kill and clean that many all at once, and neither did he. So I told him we would try 12 of them, and to see if he could be at the Talkeetna depot with them on Saturday as I would be on the train with Paul and Bud, after picking Paul up in Anchorage at the airport.

I thought we could get off the train in Talkeetna and carry the chickens on ourselves and maybe not have to pay the charges. Milton had two boxes with six hens in each box. He handed a box to Bud and one to Paul and we got back on the train and carried them into the baggage car and the baggage man put them by the door and that was that.

When we got home, we got started butchering the chickens right away. We boiled a big pot of water to help strip the feathers off the chickens, and we kept going until nearly midnight. It had turned extremely cold by the time we got home and we were forced to butcher and pluck all those chickens in the house. The smell was horrendous and the mess was worse! I vowed to never do it again. I would gladly become a vegetarian first!

Clyde killed all the chickens and I wound up gutting them because he conveniently "forgot how". We all plucked the feathers. Bud used the heads, feet and wing feathers for baiting his traps. So far he hadn't caught anything but he had not had his traps out very long. I rendered all the fat and got a good amount of chicken "lard" for making biscuits. The hens were all tough, but were good for stewing and for soup. What a 'welcome back' for Paul!

While Paul was with us, he and Bud ran the trap lines, and enjoyed running all over the country on the snow machines, wearing out the drive belts on both of them. However, Bud caught a nice big wolverine, a pale marten and two red foxes. When it was time for the Fur Rendezvous in Anchorage in February, we sent the furs in to auction and Bud got a good price for them.

After Paul got back home to California, he was in an accident and broke his leg and a couple of fingers but he healed well. He said it was safer in Alaska!

Lassie had three cute puppies in March. Our friend Grady Allred was the cook at Curry House and he wanted all three pups. Grady came up on the train to see the puppies when they were about two weeks old and weighed about five pounds each. The kids wanted to keep them all, but we told them no – two dogs were enough. We thought we would soon have to find a new home for Lassie as well. She was having two batches of puppies a year, and it was getting harder to find homes for them. Our budget did not include vet bills to have either dog neutered, unfortunately.

June, 1972. All dressed up and ready to head to the big city of Anchorage. This was a special trip; Mary and Clyde's eighteenth Anniversary Celebration. Left to right: Debbie, Clyde, Mary, Shelley.

Debbie and Lisa were coming right along with their school work, and it was a relief to me not to have to be there every minute of the day to see that they were doing it. They were old enough by that time to follow the written instructions with minimal help from me. Life was a bit easier and I had time to keep up with correspondence and other chores like cooking, baking, mending and the many other daily tasks involved in homestead life.

Shelley and Debbie were a big help as far as the baking went, since I had taught them both how to bake bread, cakes, and cookies. They really enjoyed making meals from the "care packages" my mom sent to us from time to time with cake mixes, hamburger helpers, Rice-a-Roni and things like that we never bought. Mom did not want us to be "deprived" of what she considered necessities.

Whoever was far enough ahead in their school work got to go to Anchorage with me whenever I went for supplies, which was usually around every 4-6 weeks. If Clyde was working away from Gold Creek and near Anchorage, he would shop and send supplies up to us. One way or another, it all worked out.

***

Chapter 11   Brother Bear

The morning was very cold. It was the first day of September, and we were planning to catch the train when it came south, and spending Labor Day weekend with friends in Wasilla. Clyde got up early to build a fire, and came back to bed until the house warmed up.

Momma Black Bear and two cubs in the front garden. This picture was taken through the front window from the safety of the kitchen without the benefit of a telephoto lens. A momma bear with cubs is NOT to be trifled with!

A little later he went out to cut up some wood out by the saw mill and I went to the shower house to take a shower, at about 10:00 AM. I finished getting clean about the same time Clyde was trying to start the tractor to haul in the wood. Soon he came in the house carrying a big (and still limp) dog salmon, with teeth marks in it. It had not been dead long enough to get stiff, and he showed it to me and said, "Guess where I found this?" I said "Where?"

He replied, "I think our friend bear either left us a gift or was startled by a noise one of us made, and dropped it by the burn barrel." The barrel had not been turned over, actually for several days and was still upright when Clyde found the fish. It gives one pause to think - well, the bear could have sauntered by while I was in the shower house, and was startled by some noise I made, or perhaps while Clyde was building the fire in the wood cook stove, clanking around - but at any rate, this bear managed to be invisible, as they mostly are. This one came bearing a gift. (Pun intended.)

***

Momma bear is giving her two cubs the grand tour; this time the laundry and shower facilities. The second cub is behind the washing machine. The shower is inside the door to the right of the bears. This picture was taken out the back door real quick. If momma got upset, she could cover the distance to the back door (and the photographer, ME!) in well under a second.

The same momma and her two cubs checking out our burn barrel. Momma has her head down in the barrel, one cub to the left, and you can barely see the other on the right. We burn our garbage thoroughly by frequent burning, and piling dry firewood on top the garbage to insure a complete burn. Still, hints of smell linger, enough to prompt a curious black to tip the barrel over at times. The spots are from raindrops on the window we shot this picture through from the back kitchen window.

Chapter 12 Dangerous Strangers and Loving Neighbors

The summer of 1970 the Alaska State land office made available open-to-entry five acre parcels for lease or purchase. The parcels were located in several places over quite a distance up and down the railroad.

Suddenly we had people getting off the trains right in front of our house all summer long. That would have been fine except some of them were unsavory characters – hippies, unwashed and rough edged. Many of them had alcohol and drugs; all of them had guns. Some had down filled sleeping bags, and much better camping equipment than we could ever afford, and they were living on welfare and food stamps. They also left everything they couldn't carry on or under our foot bridge making our front yard look like a dump.

There was a period of time that summer when as many as 75 people were wandering around in the woods in our valley. Most were men. Two of these characters even threatened our son in a roundabout way. When he saw them staring in the windows, he went outside to speak with them. He was not quite 14 then, and he simply informed them they were trespassing. One of the men took out a switchblade knife, snapped it open and began nonchalantly paring his fingernails with it, and said with a sneer, "Yeah? So what?"

Well, no one threatens my children and I had happened to hear this, so I right away strapped on my .44 magnum and marched outside and said in a loud and threatening way, "GET OFF MY LAND", with my right hand resting on the butt of the gun. Now, I've never shot anyone nor even pointed a gun at anyone - but they didn't know that! They left with no further trouble.

The next day two people got off; I believe their names were Bob Durr and his twelve year old son Jonathan. After the incident with the switchblade knife, I wasn't taking any chances. I marched down the path as they were coming up the path and said, "WHAT DO YOU WANT?" in a very mean way. Bob Durr said they wanted to know where the open-to-entry land was. So I pointed south, and said "About 20 miles that way." I had my gun strapped on, same as the day before and it worked. They got back on the next train and told everybody on that train what a mean woman lived here at Sherman.

Actually, Mr. Durr and his son were very nice people, and they took out land about 20 miles south, at Chase. I felt kind of bad about that.

Don Sheldon, a legendary bush pilot out of Talkeetna, told us that from the air it looked like a garbage dump up on top of the mountains behind us, where all the stuff the land seekers had brought was left. There were sheets of plastic, sleeping bags, guns and dirty clothes. It was a miracle they did not burn down the woods. Only three people actually did lease land and build cabins, but no one stayed. Thankfully, all the rest of the people who were wandering around left as soon as it got cold and snowed.

The two with the switchblade had actually moved in to our little hunting cabin we had built about halfway up the mountain (in my first book: "Journey To A Dream"). We asked the State land office if we could be held liable, should they happen to start a forest fire while living in our little cabin. They said that we would be responsible for any fire damage and would have to pay, and recommended that we go at once and tear it down which we promptly did.

They had left all their stuff - guns and all - in our little cabin. We stacked everything neatly on the ground, covered it all up with plastic, and tore down the little cabin and hauled all the logs down the hill on the Ranger. We tried to number the logs so that we could rebuild it as a shed or guest cabin but we never did. Eventually some of the logs were used in the new woodshed, the rest was cut up into firewood As far as we know, those two never came back, nor did the rest of them, except for the few who actually did take out land.

Our hunting cabin up on the mountain behind the homestead. From left to right: Shelley, Debbie, Mary, Lisa and my sister Beth.

One couple, Marcy and David Cushing were very nice, and lived at their place for several years. Marcy was a nurse and David worked in construction, I think. They moved to Petersburg where they had two boys and raised them there. They came back to see us in 2008 and to check and see if their place was still standing. It was, and no one had bothered it. It had been 30 years since they had left! It was good to see them again.

Later on Shannon Cartwright and her husband Gary bought a parcel of land from one of the folks who actually and legally had the deed, and they were my neighbors for nearly 20 years. Their place was about three miles back in the hills. Shannon is an artist and author. She illustrates children's books which she also writes. Gary is a licensed professional guide, and makes incredible jewelry and beautiful wood carvings. Shannon's newest book, "Finding Alaska", tells all about their life in the bush. They would come down to meet the train whenever Shannon had art work to mail off and we would get to see all her wonderful original art before it went into a book or poster. We would have tea and cookies if I had any baked, and visit. We certainly miss their visits. She always had her beautiful dog, Cirrus, with her. They recently moved to a place with easier access farther up the tracks. We miss them, but every once in a while we get to meet, whenever Shannon and I arc doing a book signing at the same place and time. That makes it fun.

***

At the cabin site. The roof of the cabin is on the right. The trusty Ranger was reliable transportation along the steep and in some places, treacherous path up the mountain. From left to right: Beth, Lisa, Clyde, Mary, Bud, Debbie (almost hidden in the tall grass) and Shelley.

Chapter 13 Love and Loss, Joy and Tragedy

When our daughter Shelley was almost eighteen, she entered a convent. She felt she had a vocation to life as a religious. She spent a year researching and writing to different convents all over the country. From the convents that answered, she chose the Sisters of Notre Dame in Ohio. So very far away! A month before her 18th birthday Shelley and Clyde flew to California and were met by my mother, who was thrilled to have a vocation in the family. They stayed with Mom in San Diego for a week, and Shelley got to go to Castro Valley to visit her Lovel cousins there; went to see my brother Bobby Zee in a live performance at a nightclub in San Diego, and got to experience Disneyland, Knotts Berry Farm, Sea World and the famous Wax Museum in San Francisco.

Clyde even took her down to the beach and showed her the Coronado Hotel Ballroom where he proposed to me during my senior prom. It was a magical vacation for her, full of things she had never experienced before. She was still set on going to the convent, and she, Clyde and my mother drove across the country to Ohio, and saw her settled into the convent on February 14, 1973.

It was wrenching to my heart, she was gone and we missed her so! Our oldest baby, so far from home, and the first of the four to fly the nest. She hadn't finished high school, but got her GED before she left Alaska. She attended Notre Dame College for Women in Cleveland, then Marymount School of Practical Nursing in Garfield Heights, Ohio. She seemed to be very happy and fulfilled.

Shelley was gone for almost two years, and we all missed her too much. We had been saving money for airfare and finally in 1974 the five of us flew out to see her. The Sisters of Notre Dame were very nice, putting us up in their guest house, a very comfortable house on the vast grounds of the mother house. We had a wonderful visit, and met some of the other parents of girls that were there. We were invited to dinner at one of the family's homes in Pennsylvania, across the border just a few miles from the convent. They lived so close they could see their daughter often. That trip was really pleasant and enlightening.

Later, when we were living in California, Shelley was given permission by her Mother Superior to come

visit us. She was homesick for us all, and missed Alaska. During that visit, she got to ride Lisa's horse, Lux, and also got to ride on the back of Bud's motorcycle. We had pictures of her in her habit on horseback and visiting

Shelley and Lisa, Shelley is riding Lisa's horse, Lux.

the zoo. It was good to have her with us, even if only for a short visit.

During her time in the convent, Shelley worked at various jobs. Her favorite was caring for the elderly and infirm sisters in the convent infirmary. In the fall of 1980, she was working as the school secretary and substitute teacher at the elementary school at St. Mary's Avon. After much soul searching and many months of consulting with her spiritual directors, Shelley decided not to take her final vows. She had been there for eight years before she left - we were happy that there was such a long period of adjustment, giving the women who entered that life a good solid chance to know if they were really meant for that vocation or not. (We say that she 'kicked the habit'!)

After Debbie graduated from Grossmont College in San Diego she moved back to Alaska. Bud and Lisa stayed in San Diego. Clyde and I moved to Wisconsin, as did Shelley. She worked at the VA hospital in Madison. My mother introduced her to Tim Finley at a church dance a year later. They dated for the month of December, Tim proposed on New Year's Eve and they were married in May, 1982. They lived in Madison for a few months, then Tim got the opportunity of a lifetime, to study for his Master's in organic chemistry at the University of Wyoming. After graduation they moved to the Quad Cities in Iowa.

In 1991 Shelley and Tim moved to Alaska with their four children and another on the way. At first they were apartment managers in Mountain View, then Tim got a job on the North Slope working as a chemist in the oilfields. They had six beautiful children altogether: Rachel, Timmy, Christa, Michael, Danny and Greg.

Tim continues to work on the North Slope; Shelley has worked at the Pioneer Home and Providence Extended Care Center as a nurse, taking time off for the birth of the last two boys. She is very active in her church and she also writes. They live in Eagle River.

On June 1, 2006, Michael Finley died in his sleep at the age of seventeen. It was a huge shock to our family. He had worked late the night before and afterward attended a party at a friend's house. Apparently there was a lot of music and a lot of alcohol. Michael walked home from the party in the cold rain, not feeling the cold. He went directly to his room and fell sound asleep, snoring loudly. His mom came down and pulled off his wet things, covered him snugly with a warm quilt and kissed him good night. It was ascertained by blood tests that he died of alcohol poisoning. However, his mom noted there was no alcohol odor on him, just cold rain. Michael is buried in the family cemetery at Sherman. It was not supposed to be that way. Clyde and I should have been the first ones buried there.

Clyde and I had been on the local train coming home from a trip to town for supplies, on that fateful day, the first of June. We had no idea what had happened, and had no way of knowing until we got home to Sherman, about two hours later than usual due to some problem with the tracks. When we got to the house, our radio telephone was ringing and our youngest daughter, Lisa, told us the bad news. Lisa had already called the dispatcher to ask if someone could get the message to us and get us back to town as soon as possible. Meanwhile, three men in a large rail truck on the railroad tracks stopped in front of our house, got off the truck and came up our path to ask us if they could help in any way and to tell us that we were to catch the southbound Express train back to Talkeetna in about thirty minutes. They helped load all our baggage and supplies into the house, and then left. We had time only to lock up once again after putting away any perishables, and catch the train. The conductor was very nice, and we were left alone to mourn as we rode. They let us off right where we had parked our vehicle in Talkeetna, so we could get right to Shelley and Tim's house in Eagle River.

My friend Nancy met us with sandwiches and sodas and fruit so we would not have to stop anywhere to eat. It was a terrible time for the entire family. Michael's funeral was held in St. Andrew's Catholic Church in Eagle River a few days later. Over 200 of Michael's friends, all kids his age, were there. We all pray they learn something from this tragedy. All the years we have lived in Sherman, the Alaska Railroad has been our lifeline, as it has been for everyone who lives in this 55 mile stretch with no road access. It is truly 'The Railroad with a Heart.'

***

Chapter 14 Furry Best Friends

The same summer Shelley decided to leave home, Bud wanted to try boarding out and go to a 'real school', so he could have higher math and participate in sports, (and, I suspected, meet girls.) He first went to East High in Anchorage for the second semester of his sophomore year in the spring of 1973. We arranged for him to board with Doug and Marie Dunn and family, and paid for his board. We had been under the impression that the Correspondence Study program took care of all that, but were denied, even though they did pay for Native students to board out. It was a strain on our finances, for sure, and I called many people involved with the Correspondence Study program. It seemed to me that it was discrimination if they would only pay for Native children to board out, but not white kids.

Finally after that first semester we got permission to transfer Bud to Susitna Valley High School, for his junior and senior years. The State would pay for his board and room, and we lost another kid. Debbie decided to try it too. At least Bud and Debbie were able to come home weekends. It does, after all, only cost the State one tenth the amount to educate a child by correspondence study than to have one enrolled in an actual physical school.

That winter, instead of Clyde working at Gold Creek, which was only five miles north of the homestead, he was sent to Curry, ten miles south of the homestead, to be track patrolman for the winter. The only problem with that job was that he would not be able to come home. He had to spend seven days a week there, to take care of the two big diesel generators as well as patrolling. The patrolman's quarters were upstairs and the rent was $56 a month. Clyde got permission to move us to Curry as well. The week after Christmas we moved and were there until May, when we moved back home.

By that time we had no more rabbits, and had found a good home for Lassie. So we packed Copper, our cat named Elmer, all the clothes and Lisa's school books and moved to Curry. We had automatic heat, hot and cold running water, indoor plumbing, electricity and best of all, a refrigerator. What a treat.

We had been so used to living without those things, when we had them again, we all got lazy. Lisa had her own room, and of course Clyde and I had our room. When Bud and Debbie came for weekends, there were rooms available for them, as well. The apartment was nice and was mostly furnished so we didn't have to bring much, only a few dressers and two beds. There was a small living room, a medium sized kitchen, a real bathroom with a big claw foot tub and a shower as well. What luxury!

We missed our own home and the peace and quiet we were used to. Still, we were all together, the three of us, and on weekends, Bud and Debbie were with us. We missed Shelley even more and wished she were there with us. But we wrote her copious letters and she wrote back of course and seemed happy and content where she was.

Curry in 1969. There used to be a thriving town of over 300 here when the railroad still used steam engines. Presently there is nothing remaining of the old town of Curry except a log cabin across the track that was the ski chalet. This building was originally the military barracks and was converted into a mess hall for serving the trainmen on freight trains. It has since been torn down by the railroad. We had the apartment to the far left upstairs. The generator shed is just out of the picture to the right. The mighty Susitna River is in the background.

It was noisy there at Curry with the generators going 24 hours a day. The shed housing the generators was about 20 feet from the tracks. Curry House was about 100 feet from the tracks, much closer than our home, which is 310 feet away. It made a big difference, the building being closer to the tracks. The trains going by were noisy and vibrated the building. It took us awhile to get used to it all so we could finally get a good night's sleep.

Copper began scratching and digging at his nose and sneezing. We thought he had an infection, perhaps from an old porcupine quill we might have missed. When Clyde was able, he took Copper to the nearest veterinarian, in Palmer. The vet anesthetized him so deeply that it took 48 hours for him to wake up. He said it was necessary to put him out so that he could take an X-ray of Copper's nose. The X-ray showed nothing, and Clyde brought Copper back to Curry. He stayed unconscious, and when he finally did come to, he was so disoriented he bumped into walls, fell over, could not eat, only drank water. I called the vet to tell him of this and ask what we should do and all he said was "Oh, he probably has distemper". A couple of days later Copper began having convulsions.

By the time Bud came home on the weekend, Copper had lost so much weight, was no better at all. Since he was Bud's dog, Bud took him out to the upstairs landing at Curry house and shot him after talking to him a long time and holding him. It was so hard for him to do that; he did not tell us he was going to, he just did it. We were all so upset. Copper was barely ten years old, and probably would not have lived much longer anyway, but we wished we had never taken him to that vet since we found out later that that vet was not any good. Copper had never been sick a day in his life. It hurt us so much we decided not to have any more pets. And Clyde and I have not had any more pets of our own, but our kids all have dogs and cats and we share. If we have a mouse problem, we borrow one of the cats for awhile, usually Andre, who loves it up here and was a great mouser until she got asthma. Now she wheezes so much when she is hunting it scares all the mice and birds away. When any of the kids come to visit, they usually bring their pets.

Lisa has a huge beautiful Akita, Buke, as well as two cats, Andre and Dougie. Andre is a great outdoors cat, she loves to hunt. But Dougie is only happy indoors and if he ever sees a mouse, it is just something to play with.

Left to right: Buke, Andre and Doug, the Larmi family's pets.

On Memorial Day weekend, 2002, Lisa, Eugene, and Buke came up for the weekend along with a couple of their friends. We left so they could have the place all to themselves and we visited with some friends in Wasilla. That weekend, Lisa and Gene were walking down the railroad tracks with Buke, when along came the RDC, our little local train.

Buke saw that train coming at him, and immediately went into attack mode. He had never seen a train coming at him before; it was our self-propelled local train, affectionately called the Budd Can, because the cars were made by the Budd company. Lisa could not get hold of Buke and neither could Gene, without getting hit by the train themselves, and the train could not stop in time, so it hit Buke and sent him end over end under both cars. When it had passed completely over him, Buke got up and staggered off to the nearest snow pile and laid down in the snow. Lisa was sure he was mortally hurt but she and Gene ran over to him, and Lisa sat down and put Buke's bleeding head on her lap and began examining him as best she could. Soon Buke got up and began slowly walking toward the house, every once in a while laying down in a pile of snow. It was spring, of course, but not all the snow was gone. There were occasional piles here and there where it had drifted deeply. The rest of the ground was bare.

The RDC, which stands for Rail Diesel Car. It is more like a bus than a train; each car is self contained with two diesel engines, a baggage area, a passenger area, and of course the place for the engineer.

They finally made it to the house and cleaned Buke up as well as they could. A few hours later they caught the southbound RDC to Wasilla and took poor Buke to an animal hospital where the doctor examined him thoroughly and could find no broken bones. But there was a lot of hide torn off and a big long creosote splinter running up inside his skin in the side of his face almost to his eye. He had lots of black grease ground into his fur and all the hair and skin around his back end under his tail was ripped off and gravel ground in. He was only a year old, without much sense - but he lived to tell the tale. One of the few animals ever hit by a train to live. He is fine now, except for some arthritis in his hips. The train conductor and engineer were astounded that he had lived at all, and of course they felt really bad about running him over, but there was no way to stop the train. The animal doctor had kept Buke overnight for observation; x-rays showed no broken bones. But he was one sore dog for quite some time. His picture was taken the day after he got out of the animal hospital, with the protective collar on and not all of the grease and creosote gone.

Shelley has a cat, and until recently, she also had a

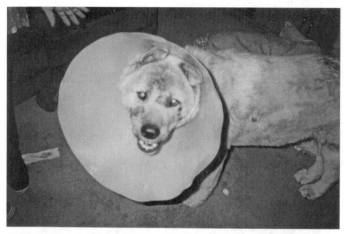

Buke after the vet fixed him up. We still tell Lisa she sure has one 'well trained' dog!

dog. Fawn was a beautiful golden retriever, and she too, loved coming to the homestead whenever Shelley and family came up. She was very much an outdoor dog until she got older, but still loved it. One day last winter she went out into the back yard of the Finley family home in Eagle River, lay down in the snow, and fell asleep. She never woke up. She was 12 years old or more and had had a good life. She is sorely missed by all her family.

Debbie and family have two cats: Arthur and Jane. Both are big cats and beautiful. Arthur is dark gray and white and has long hair. Jane is an orange tabby. She is shy, timid, and beautiful but friendly.

Bud and his family have two dogs and a cat. The cat is really Cynthia's, our daughter-in-law. His name is Van. He is a long haired pale golden beautiful kitty, but not real friendly. The dog Achilles, or Keeley for short, is pretty, smart and a lively pup about a year old, half Lab and half Husky, and he belongs to Amanda, Bud's daughter. The older dog, Houdini, or Dini for short, is a medium size black Karelian Bear Dog, and blind since she was about one year old. However, she is happy and gets around well, knows her territory and one cannot tell she is blind, usually. She and Keeley both love coming to the homestead.

***

Dini

Amanda and Achilles

Van. He is a Turkish Van breed.

Chapter 15 Off To Worship

When Bud started school in Talkeetna at Susitna Valley High School in the fall of 1973, he was a junior. We had not yet moved to Curry. He got on the varsity basketball team, and we managed to go to several games when the weather wasn't too bad. Once by snow machine, and once by gas car. We were lucky to get a ride to the high school both times.

We didn't own a car and usually did not need one. Whenever we went to Anchorage by train, we were either picked up by friends at the depot or we took a cab and stayed at a motel. We had several friends in Anchorage who loved coming up for weekends or longer, and we were always welcome at their homes, which was nice. But when we had family or friends coming from the States, we always stayed at a motel.

We stayed about five months at Curry this time, and it was a nice break from the hard work of homestead life. We had been short of firewood for the winter - Clyde had put in such long hours he did not get a chance to cut enough. Also we were having problems getting gasoline and propane shipped up on the freight; it seemed there was some sort of shortage going on at that time.

We were also able to get to Talkeetna and go to church sometimes. It was 10 miles closer than from the homestead. We had only found out there was a Catholic church in Talkeetna the last time we were in Anchorage for supplies and went to church there. A nun told us where the church was in Talkeetna, and that there was a resident priest there. It was called St. Bernard's. She gave me the priest's name and phone number and when we got back from Anchorage I called him and told him where we lived and how the trains ran and how difficult it was to get to church, etc.

His name was Father Stanley Allie. He had a plane since he had so many miles to travel between parishes but it only had wheels, not floats or skis, and he could not land on small bush strips. But, he said that any time we could get to Talkeetna, any day or night, he would say Mass for us.

The first time we went to Mass at St. Bernard's, Bud took the snow machine with the sled attached, Clyde took the gas car and the girls and I caught the train. When we got off the train, Clyde and Bud had been there for an hour already, but Clyde could not leave the gas car with all the railroad equipment. So the girls and I piled on the snow machine and sled and Bud drove us the few blocks to the church. Father Allie was just getting in his car to deliver a package of medicine to someone, and he showed us into his house, turned on the TV, and told us to make ourselves at home, that he would be back in twenty minutes. He was back in fifteen.

We talked for several minutes, and then went next door to the church and he showed us around. It was a small church with folding metal chairs. All the walls and open peaked ceiling were pine paneled. He told us that the entire town used the church as a town hall. Every Friday the church was turned into either a movie theater or a bingo hall. Even a kitchen was attached and the people of Talkeetna donated a Hammond organ to the church. The town had suppers and socials there also. It didn't look much like a church to me until Father Allie proceeded to the front wall and moved a different looking wood panel to the side. He explained that the entire wall came out in panels and was closed up when the church was being used as a hall. He said he wouldn't remove all the panels; we could just come on in and sit around the altar.

Inside the paneled part was a raised platform that was carpeted, with the altar, candles, and a large beautiful crucifix on the wall behind the altar; the baptismal font over to one side, the tabernacle on the other. The four of us had our own private Mass grouped around the altar. It was very nice and very different. Afterward, we thanked Father Allie kindly and had to get back to the depot.

Poor Clyde was worried, didn't know where to find us, couldn't leave his gas car to look for us and was late, so he had to extend his lineup, which he didn't want to do. He was new on the job, and not supposed to transport women and kids on the gas car. He and Bud loaded the barrel of gas he had bought on the sled and Bud took off on the snow machine pulling the gas behind him.

Clyde got on the dispatch phone and extended his lineup until 9:30 PM with no problem, which soothed his ruffled nerves a bit. The girls and I piled into that dinky gas car with Clyde and we took off for the 32 mile ride to Sherman. And brrr! Was it ever cold!!! We just about froze to death before we got home at 9:00 PM. Clyde, Bud and I turned the gas car around and Clyde drove the 10 miles back to Curry and tied up for the night, just in time. He stayed at Curry. We still had wood, kindling and coal to get in, and fires to build.

I had made a huge pot of chili that morning so all we had to do was heat it up for our dinner. Sure helped to warm us up. We were all worn out. That's what I considered a supreme effort to get to church! Should help make up for all the times we missed when we could have gone. When we were actually living at Curry, we made it more often to church, but certainly not every week. It was just too risky getting there and back.

The following summer, we were back at home in Sherman. Father Allie brought a big group with him: the ladies of the church and the St. Bernard's CYO teens from Talkeetna on the train. It was a gorgeous sunny day and we had Mass in the front yard. I really think God understands.

***

Chapter 16 Education and State Government

We planted our garden, though smaller in size, and had a fairly good summer even though Clyde was gone being relief foreman at Ferry, which is over one hundred and thirteen miles north of the homestead, and also at Whittier most of the summer. Whittier is about sixty miles south of Anchorage, and you have to go through one really long and one pretty long tunnel to get there. While he was at Ferry, he phoned us one day and while I was talking to him, I heard him drop the phone and yell. Then there was a bunch of noise, and finally he came back on the line and told me a bear had just pushed open the screen door and walked right into the section house. When he yelled, it scared the bear enough so that he ran out again. Clyde immediately shut the door and locked it, and told me to send up the rifle on the train along with his sleeping bag, which he had forgotten to pack. I sent up all he had asked for that day, when the train came.

He was assigned to Curry again in early fall. As soon as the garden was all harvested and the canning all done, we moved back for the winter again. It was not hard to move back, since we had done it once already. We saved a bunch on fuel and wood for heat. We were saving up for another trip to Ohio to see Shelley once again. But God had other plans.

Debbie was on her last year of high school by correspondence. She had attended Susitna Valley High for her sophomore and junior years. When it came time to start her senior year, she was short by a quarter credit by Mat-Su Borough requirements, so she decided to do her senior year by correspondence. She did get to graduate in 1976 with her class at Susitna Valley High School.

Lisa was in the eighth grade. In February Lisa was elected as a delegate by the eighth grade class (53 in the class), none of whom had met each other except through the yearly journal, called "Scattered Chatter". She was to represent the eighth grade class on a trip to Juneau where she would finally get to meet the teachers and those who worked at the Correspondence Study School. I was called on the phone and asked if I could come too, as I had been teaching the kids for 11 years and they would like me to give my views on correspondence study. They paid our plane fare. We thought that would be fun to do and we left on the train to Anchorage on February 4th, and left Sunday morning on a plane to Juneau. We returned to Anchorage on Thursday, and home on the train again Saturday. We were gone for 10 days altogether and were excited about our mini vacation. It was fun, except for the fright of flying sideways between the mountains to get to Juneau through the skinny pass there between the high mountain peaks. What a scary thing!!

The kids who went drew up a constitution for the school which they had never had before. They got to visit the State Capitol, see how government is run, and ask many questions. I thought it was a splendid idea and a great learning tool for all of us. There were three delegates from high school and one from eighth grade.

Debbie stayed home to keep house and cook for her dad. We bought her some very pretty things as a reward for all her work. Even though it was not much work to keep house there in Curry! Lisa and I finally got to meet all her teachers and some of her school mates. Lisa stayed with one of her teachers, as most of the kids did, and I shared a hotel room with Alice Posey, a very nice lady and correspondence mother. We got to be friends and corresponded quite frequently for a time.

We had an intense three full days of meeting with the other mothers, and all the teachers, discussing the courses and how we thought they could be improved, what to keep, what to leave out, and we four mothers were then an official advisory board in the interest of all our kids to see they got the best there was. We planned lots of things for our kids to do, get-togethers, swimming lessons, life saving courses, camping trips, all things where they could get with and meet other kids in their grades, also on correspondence study.

For all those years we had had nothing and all of a sudden it seemed we were finally going places. This was all to encourage kids to keep on with correspondence study rather than leave home to board out for school; to improve the high school courses so they would get more from them, to have Alaska oriented courses, vocational courses, better everything for our kids.

At that time the State of Alaska took the view that it would rather localize correspondence study. We felt this ridiculous, and that it would make the whole thing fall apart, and all to the detriment of our kids.

The students went to the Capital Building and sat in on a session of debate one morning. Mrs. Posey and I were able to go the next morning. She and I were flying back to Anchorage the next evening. Lisa stayed on until Monday, horseback riding (indoor rink), swimming (Indoor pool) and staying with Mrs. J. who had a daughter (also horse crazy) and Lisa's age. She had a great time. The two girls went to a junior high school dance Friday afternoon. Although it was snowing, Juneau was beautiful.

Bud graduated from Susitna Valley High School right on schedule in 1975, in the top two percent of the nation, academically. There were nine people in his graduating class. Bud, at 6' 2", was the second tallest in his class, with his friend Ben Porterfield topping him by about four inches! We all attended the graduation exercises. Bud went on to the University of Alaska in Fairbanks and we did not see him until the Christmas break when he came home (by train), to spend the holidays with us. It was a great Christmas, except we all still missed Shelley. Her absence left such a gap!

Debbie graduated with her class at Susitna Valley High school the following year, 1976 and went to work in Anchorage as an au pair for the summer. That left only three of us. Our house felt very empty. We moved back to Sherman once again early in the spring. Someone with more seniority outbid Clyde for the patrolman job, so he was once again working at Gold Creek

***

Mary, Bud and Clyde at Bud's Highs School Graduation

From left to right: Lisa, Bud, Ben Porterfield, and Debbie

Chapter 17 California Here We Come!

That spring, when the tracks were mostly bare of snow, Clyde took his Terra Torque (fat wheeled motorized two wheel bike) up the tracks to work. He was sure the snow was gone enough that he could make it. But he hit a patch of ice, and his bike flipped over and down the bank almost all the way into the river. Clyde held on though, and managed to save the bike and wrestled it back up the bank and proceeded on to work. This happened twice, and by the time he got to work, late, he was exhausted and could hardly move. Seems he had done major damage to his back, and each day it got worse.

He finally went to Anchorage to see a doctor and the doctor said there was nothing he could do for him. He had no broken bones, just torn tissues and muscle and tendon damage, lots of it, and he should see a specialist. Same answer from the specialist.

He went to the railroad doctor and his opinion was that Clyde should go for a medical retirement, that he would never be able to do track work again, his back was such a wreck. Clyde also had considerable hearing loss. The doctor recommended he retire on his hearing loss, since it was easier to show than the damage to his back. He told Clyde that what he needed to do was to move somewhere with enough doctors to help him. There certainly were not enough in Alaska!! This was early in the spring of 1976. By late August, we had most things in place for our move.

Clyde continued to work, if you can call it that. All he did was shamble down the path each morning and, with help, get on the gas car and sit there and ride around all day in excruciating pain, get off the gas car at night and shamble up the path to the house and go to bed. It was not a nice life.

Lisa and I packed and sorted and threw away. Clyde, through his friends and word of mouth, managed to sell some of our hard earned equipment, the Gravely, the Ranger, garden tiller, and a few other odds and ends. Debbie had been working in Anchorage and came home to help. She wasn't happy with her job, working in the Room Service for the Westward Hilton, and decided to come to California with us. She wanted to go on to college.

We had discussed where to go and with my family's help found that there were plenty of good doctors in California, so that is where we went. Clyde could not leave until his retirement went through, but the girls and I got on a plane with as much luggage as we could take, and flew to San Diego where my sister Kathy met us at the airport. This was in late August 1976.

We had just enough time to register the girls in school, Lisa at Monte Vista High School and Debbie at Grossmont Community College, and find a place to rent. Meanwhile we were crammed in with my sister Kathy in her little house with her husband Dave and their son little David.

Within a week I found, with Kathy's help, a house to rent in Spring Valley. The rent wasn't too bad, but I didn't have enough money for first and last month's rent and cleaning deposit, and made a deal with the landlord to clean up the previous tenant's mess in lieu of a cleaning deposit if he would just let us rent from month to month, payment in advance. That is what we did. We didn't expect the mess we found. There was rotten food in the refrigerator, sacks of garbage in the service porch, living room and all of it was full of cockroaches. Ugh! But for three days we sprayed and cleaned and scrubbed and finally got rid of the roaches and the mess – seven truckloads of garbage - and by that time the things we had shipped down came, so we moved in.

Little by little we furnished the house, with mostly used garage sale stuff. There was a big fenced back yard, and, (after talking it over with me) Kathy gave Lisa her wonderful trail horse, named Lux, along with a pole corral for her sixteenth birthday. Lisa was ecstatic, since she had always wanted a horse. We installed Lux at the bottom of the yard, and Lisa would let him out daily to graze on the lawn while she cleaned the corral. She rode him nearly every day after school.

The first day of school, Lisa came home and said, "Mom, the kids at school are SO Immature! It's like being with a bunch of little grade school kids!" I thought then, what have we done to our kids? People used to tell me, on the train when they found out our kids did not go to school, that we were depriving them of being with their peers, that by keeping them at home, that we were stunting them somehow. I stopped feeling guilty about that long ago, but once again I wondered if we had damaged our kids somehow. The work was easy for Lisa, and she got straight A's all the way through high school.

My brother Bobby had an old Plymouth that ran, but not well, and he gave that to me. He had just bought a Ford Ranchero, which he needed to haul around his music equipment to the different places he and his band were playing. I agreed to pay him a small sum for the car when I had money coming in, and Lisa agreed to buy hay and grain for Lux with babysitting money just as soon as she got any babysitting jobs.

Brother-in-law Dave worked on the car and got it into better running condition, except it used an awful lot of oil. We smoked our way down the road.

Meanwhile, I had to get a job of some sort, but I wasn't qualified for anything, since I had only a high school diploma, and no college. I couldn't even be a teacher's aide, even though I had taught my own children for 12 years. Debbie and I applied for a grant through the RETC Program. We attended a school called Eaton College of Business. We took classes in medical office procedures and terminology. The program was eight hours a day, five days a week and lasted for three months. On weekends, I cleaned houses for food money, and we got by. After we finished our program at Eaton College, we both were able to get jobs in medical offices.

We had been in San Diego since the 26th of August, and Clyde finally made it by October 2nd. He was in terrible shape, and we hastened to get him to a doctor as soon as possible. He actually wound up having several doctors, all of whom helped him somewhat. It took an entire year of him sleeping on the floor, physical therapy, traction, and pain pills, but finally he got to where he could move without excruciating pain.

Eventually he went to work also at whatever he could find that was physically easy starting with half days only and working his way up to a full day. It all took time.

Debbie enrolled in Grossmont College and earned her Associate of Arts in Ceramics in 1980. She did very well, and we were very proud of her. Lisa graduated from Monte Vista High School that same spring. Both girls wanted to go back to Alaska, and so did we, but at that time my mother was living in Wisconsin. She had moved there the year before we came, and had a job as a volunteer social worker, finding adoptive homes for unwanted infants. She loved her job and was content. She had just bought a house, which needed all kinds of work, and asked if Clyde and I could come out there to help her for a bit. We sold everything we could and Lisa stayed in California, Debbie went to Alaska and we went to Wisconsin. We kept in close touch.

***

Chapter 18 Blessed With Children, Grandchildren And Our First Great Grandchild!

In 1978 two years after we moved to California, Bud came from Alaska to where we were at that time, and apprenticed at a fine furniture building shop. While he was there, he met Diane, and they were together for some time. Eventually they married. Bud moved back to Alaska about a year after Debbie moved back, and Diane followed him. They had a tempestuous marriage, but did manage to have four beautiful children, Jackie, Nathan, Amanda and Vanessa. Eventually they agreed to disagree and got a divorce.

Jackie at her graduation from The Masters Collage in May, 2004

Nathan at the homestead, age 17, summer 2004 Having a great time helping Bud and Clyde with getting logs for the sawmill.

Christmas, 2004. Vanessa, age 11, helping Grandma Mary bake bread and other Christmas goodies.

Amanda at the homestead, age 16, 2008 She is washing dishes in the sink out back with the gravity flow water (ice cold!) from the creek, and picking cranberries on right.

Two years after the divorce, Bud was back in California taking a course for his construction job on how to run the Master Builder™ software, a complicated computer program. He met a lovely woman named Cynthia Lewis. She was the training manager for the software company. Although at that time Bud had sworn he would never marry again, Cynthia struck a chord in his heart and they became friends at once. One thing led to another and finally Cynthia came to Alaska to check it out, never having been here before. She fell in love with the place, and agreed to move up here to live. Bud found her an apartment, and Cynthia quickly found a job teaching computer science. Not long after that, they were married and now live in Wasilla.

Cynthia and Bud on their wedding day, May, 1997

Bud's two oldest children, Jackie and Nathan, are grown and have flown the nest. Jackie is married to Jeremy Powell and they live in California. They have recently given birth to our first great-grandchild, Brayden David Powell.

At this writing, we have yet to meet him. Nathan is twenty one now, and lives in Anchorage where he works. Bud's two youngest daughters, (Amanda, 18 and Vanessa, 17) live with Bud and Cynthia in Wasilla. They all come as often as they can to Sherman to enjoy the homestead.

Brayden Powell, our first Great-grandchild. He is one week old in this picture with his momma, our granddaughter Jackie and daddy, Jeremy

***

Chapter 19 Going Back Home to Sherman

While we were living Outside, in Wisconsin, I longed for the peace and quiet of Sherman. It was very different in Wisconsin, as it was in California, but it was not home! Oh, it was great to be with my mom again, and we made many new friends both in California and in Wisconsin. We had a great garden there, many tomatoes and lots of corn, peppers, melons, all stuff we could not grow in Alaska. But oh, it wasn't Alaska!! Mom's house was so small it was perfect for her, but crowded with us there.

We bought the big house next door to Mom's and moved all three of us in there so Clyde and other people he got to help him could fix Mom's house. It needed plumbing, wiring, insulating, (it had lathe and plaster walls inside; the house was about 80 years old.) It needed wallboard, reinforcing of floors, and repairs to the porch.

Mom talked Clyde into remodeling the storage shed attached to the house into an efficiency apartment with a tiny kitchen, bathroom; basically a one room living space. She wanted it for a rental unit for income. It turned out really cute, and Mom had no problem keeping it rented. The main part of Mom's house came out fine as well.

Clyde's brother, Glen, drove up to Wisconsin one day from Missouri and told us he was on his way to Alaska, and asked us if we wanted to come along. He had never been there. He had his girlfriend and her brother with him. We jumped at the chance, and Shelley came too, and we agreed to pay half of the gas and for our food. And so we left, and camped out in tents all the way home. They had a truck with a camper, with just barely room enough for the three of them. It was a crowded ride, but we made it at last. It was the summer of 1981. We stayed home for a month, and then the three of us flew back. Glen and company did not like it in Alaska and left almost immediately.

It was so hard for us to leave to go back to Wisconsin, but Shelley had to get back for her job, and we had a bit of stuff to finish up for Mom, but we vowed to move back home just as soon as ever we could. Our poor little house in Sherman needed quite a bit of work, since the roof had leaked while we were gone and the foundation was dry rotting, the floor sagging, and it was in sad shape.

In 1982 we came home to Alaska for the entire summer. Debbie was between jobs and came home to recuperate. Clyde worked with Bud on several of his construction jobs, in Anchorage, and we made what repairs we could to keep the house from falling in. Debbie and I enjoyed our time together at home.

That summer, Mark and Lee, biologists for the Alaska Department of Fish and Game, were up and down the Susitna river counting fish and putting tags and radios on them and writing environmental reports for the proposed Susitna Dam project. They had a neat jet boat with depth sounder and everything. One day they stopped and came up to the house. I think they could smell the fresh bread baking all the way down to the river. At any rate, we fed them, and told them we wished that we could get across the river to the 4th of July creek over there where we knew the fishing was good, because we needed to catch just enough for a canner full. They said they would be more than happy to bring us over and even to help us catch the fish!!

After lunch, that is what we did, and they helped us too. It was lots of fun, riding in that boat. We had more than a canner full of fish, and Debbie and I spent the afternoon cleaning and canning the salmon. Meanwhile, the fish and game men told us that the rapids at Devil's Canyon did not stop the King salmon from making it up to the huge spawning pools above the rapids. They were some of the largest and most crowded spawning pools they had seen. They told us that they were making it a point to stop and tell everyone who lived anywhere near about the spawning grounds, that the powers that be kept conveniently losing all the paperwork they sent in regarding the importance of these spawning grounds.

If Devil's Canyon Dam went through, it would wipe out a huge potential for King salmon. It would warm the river and ruin many species of fish which could only live in icy waters. They also told us that where the proposed dam would be was right on top of three major earthquake faults and if there were to be a major earthquake it would wipe everything out all the way to and past Talkeetna. That if the dam were full, the water level would be more than 50 feet deep when it hit Talkeetna! If the lake that would be formed was full, it would be ten miles long five miles wide and a mile deep. I can't imagine anything that big, but everyone seemed to overlook all the danger and cost of that project and now and then someone keeps trying to resurrect the plan.

Now it would cost billions of dollars to make, and seems to me it is a useless waste of money when there are so many other possible places to put a dam for hydroelectric power where no one would be in harms way. Also all the other things there were to do, so much cheaper and ecology friendly; wind power, solar cells, etc.

***

Chapter 20 Home at Last

Spring of 1983 we finally moved home, shipping what we had to, including the big beautiful 900 pound Monarch wood cook stove which was in the kitchen of the house we bought next door to Mom's house, and whatever other stuff we needed. We had sold the house and the house money made it possible for us to finally move back home. Things have a way of working out, one way or the other. Clyde's nephew John Beckmann drove up with us, in his own car, planning to spend a year or so in Alaska. He had not been here since he was a teen-ager, when his folks, brother and two sisters spent six weeks with us that early summer of 1969, right after we got the second story built onto the house.

Bud spent part of the summer of 1983 helping us put new foundation and floors in the house at Sherman. We repainted the outside, planted a garden, and did what we could. The most important thing was, we were home again at last.

That same summer our friends Edna and Elmer Georgeson came to visit us from Wisconsin. They drove up, and spent a week with us and a week with friends of theirs they had gone to school with back in Wisconsin, who lived in Wasilla, and still do. It was Edna and Elmer's first trip to Alaska.

They made it a point to come back every summer for at least a week to spend with us, and we took various trips around the state with them. One way to see your home state is to have visitors from out of state come and then you go here and there with them, to show them around, even if you have not been there yourself!!

We loved having them and they only missed two summers coming because of other family obligations. We missed them so much when they did not make it up. We had lots of fun with them and look forward to their visits eagerly each year. Once when Edna and Elmer came to visit, we took a trip, which turned out to be outstanding for all of us. Since that time, we have taken several trips to various places in Alaska, each were unique. l will tell you about a few of them.

On one trip we took off on a gorgeous day with sunshine, a little breeze, cloudless sky. We drove to

Edna and Elmer Georgeson

Portage, a good road all the way, and lovely scenery. We parked at the waiting place on the left of the highway for boarding the train. While waiting, we sat in the sun and baked a little, getting relaxed and sleepy After awhile a girl came by each car and collected fares. The line kept getting longer and the sun continued to beat down.

We got thirsty and hungry, so I fixed lunch with the food we brought along. We had cheese sandwiches, dill pickles and potato chips. A little later we noticed people going by with hot dogs and cokes, so Clyde and Elmer went in search of something cold to drink. There was a concession stand way up past the car boarding area, near the foot passenger area, and bought us all cold cans of Coke. The snowy mountain tops shown in the sun, truly a marvelous day. The breeze was just enough to keep it cool and there was just a little dust in the air.

The line grew longer and soon became two lines of cars, including tour buses and lots of people, all of us hoping to drive aboard the ferry in Whittier and sail away to Valdez, which we were told was a seven hour boat trip with breath taking scenery and lots to do.

At last we were able to board the train. Just drove the car onto the flatbed and parked. Someone came by and chocked the wheels so we would not be able to move, and advised us to stay in the car for the entire trip, for our safety. When everyone was loaded, the train moved and we were soon in the tunnels, a weird feeling. The entire

At the Dollar Creek Mine. From left to right; Clyde, Edna, Deloris, George, Mary, and Elmer. The Dollar Creek Mine is a patented Federal gold claim owned by George and Deloris McCullough. On a bright sunny day!

trip took 15 minutes, to Whittier through the mountains, and when we stopped, someone came by and un-chocked the wheels and we drove off and on to the ferry yard. We got in line again, and when it was time, drove on to the ferry. It was relaxing, and when we got to Valdez, we drove off again and went on our way. We saw some astoundingly beautiful sights along the way and all the way back on the drive up the highway back to Anchorage.

One year we four went to Kodiak and spent the night at a bed and breakfast and spent two whole days exploring the island. It was sunny and fine. The only drawback to this trip was the fact that we had to wait about six hours in the Anchorage airport for the fog to lift on Kodiak. We wondered if we would get to fly back in time for Edna and Elmer to catch their flight home. We barely did and decided that next time we decided to visit Kodiak, we would go by boat.

Another time we drove down the Petersville Road, a horrid, bumpy, lousy road, to Dollar Creek Mine where some friends of Bud's lived. We each had campers and when we finally made it to the mine site, we panned for gold. Then we visited with George and Delores McCullough, who owned the place. Their son Pete went to school with Bud.

The last trip we took was to Skagway where we hopped aboard the narrow gage railroad train for the historic ride up the mountain. It was quite interesting and certainly beautiful scenery. The trip was narrated, told all about the gold rush days and how the railroad was built in two years, two months and two days with a crew of 30,000 (not all at once). Some of them only worked long enough to get enough money for a grubstake - they were mostly all gold seekers. We stayed at the White House, a really nice bed and breakfast place and shopped a lot and had a wonderful time.

Several months after that trip, I was doing a book signing at Annabelle's Book Store in Wasilla and met Dawson Dolly, a most entertaining woman from Skagway who, unbeknownst to us was an entertainer on the Skagway train in the 'Parlor car'. She was dressed fit to kill, all feathers and jewels and tight ruffled satin gown, big hat, long curly blonde wig, and lots of makeup, dressed in her usual role as a "madam". She had written a book and was selling it too, and I certainly enjoyed her, and her book. Hope to get to meet her again. She had to go to a real madam to learn how to act like one, she said. She is an actress.

We went to Valdez one summer with Edna and Elmer, and to Fairbanks, another time, and Denali Park. Seward was another place we visited. We have taken lots of trips to lots of places, all interesting and different. When we weren't traveling somewhere, we spent the time on the homestead. We always spent at least a week there, travel or not. Edna called it her R&R time. Elmer helped Clyde repair or rebuild whatever needed repairing or rebuilding, whether it was a roof on a shed, a broken piece of machinery or what. He helped build our "depot" down by the railroad tracks. Sometimes the weather was good, sometimes it was rainy and cool.

***

Clyde giving some of the grandkids (left to right: Michael Finley, Greg Finley, MaryAlice Larmi and Danny Finley) a ride

Chapter 21 It's *All* Airmail Now!

Back in 1983 Clyde's nephew John had come to stay for awhile and was helping cut wood, and when it snowed he set traps, planning to run a trap line He hadn't found a job in Anchorage, but had his application in many places. He decided to spend some time with us.

Winter came, as it always does, and when there was enough snow our friend Nancy came down from Gold Creek on her snow machine and hauled wood for us all afternoon - we did not have one as yet,. Clyde had been working on woodpiles out in the wood lot so we would have enough to heat the house for the winter. We had no machinery or equipment of any kind to haul it, so he, John, and I had been hauling loads on backpacks to the house - a very slow way to put in a winter supply of wood. As soon as it snowed, we used a little sled to haul the wood in, which was still slow but not as hard.

When Nancy came down from Gold Creek; we had lunch and she spent the afternoon hauling wood to the house. John stayed at the woodpile and loaded her sled and she just drove, and Clyde unloaded the sled at the woodshed and split the bigger logs and I stacked. We got all the wood in, thanks to Nancy, so Clyde cut more trees the next day and I stacked and we had three nice woodpiles out in the woods just waiting for Nancy's next trip down. We decided we must have a snow machine of our own again soon. Saw a big black wolf across the river that morning.

It was so great to be home once again and I had a wonderful time visiting with Nancy and trying to catch up on all the news - we had been gone for so very long!! For some reason, we had not written to each other very much - I guessed we were both too busy with our different lives.

We still got our mail from the train, thrown off with a rock or flashlight battery in the mail envelope so it would not blow under the train, and we mailed our outgoing mail the same way. We either gave it to the Gold

Creek foreman or to the track patrolman from Curry to put on the train, or we would put a rock in the mail envelope and toss it in the open baggage car door as the train went by.

Debbie, Lisa, and Bud were living and working in Anchorage. John, Clyde and I were the only ones at home at Sherman. John was planning to go into town soon and look for work. We were planning to go in for the Fur Rendezvous in February, (nicknamed 'Rondy') our winter celebration that goes on for 10 days with all sorts of games, plays, displays, fur auction, all over town. We had not received any mail for about 2 weeks at that time, and then suddenly, or so it seemed to us, we all got notices from the Alaska Railroad that the Post Office refused to renew the contract with them, and therefore we would no longer be receiving our mail through the Alaska Railroad.

The notice said that we should make other arrangements as soon as possible to get our mail some other way, perhaps a post office box at the nearest post office. We inquired about a post office box in Talkeetna, the nearest post office, and found out there was a waiting list for boxes, and we could wait years, possibly, before ever getting one. There was a definite problem. How could we and all the other families north of us living along the railroad get our mail?

We all depended on mail to order groceries, pay taxes and bills, keep in touch with our families, and the children living out here all went to school through correspondence study programs. Most of us didn't have phones, since the lines had all been taken down in the early '80s. The mail was our only means of keeping in touch with the 'outside' world. There was no road access at all in this area, only the Alaska Railroad. Therefore, most of our buying was done by mail order. For us, mail day was "The Big Event" of the week.

Rondy week was upon us, and we went to Anchorage on the train on Sunday to spend the week. We decided to go to the Alaska Railroad depot to pick up our mail on Monday morning and to find out what, if anything, we could do to remedy the mail situation. We were informed by a man behind the baggage counter that all mail had been returned to the Post Office, stamped "Not at this address; try Star Rte.", beginning that morning and from then on. We were advised to 'start making phone calls' if we wanted mail delivery. We were told that the Post Office refused to pay the railroad to deliver mail, and the railroad refused to do it for nothing, which they had been doing since September of 1983. It was now February 1984.

We started by calling the Post Office, of course the wrong one, and found out from that person we should call the big one at the airport, and to ask for a Mr. Benton, the Post Office supervisor. After calling about six numbers, and explaining to each person why I was calling, obtaining a different number from each one, finally Mr. Benton's secretary answered, only to inform me that "Mr. Benton was in a meeting and could not be disturbed." I left the phone number I was calling from and requested that he please call back as soon as possible.

Rather than just wait, I called Senator Ted Stevens' office, and explained the problem to his secretary, Lona Hodson. She was very helpful, and promised to inform the Senator of our plight, as soon as he returned to the office later that day. She told me that he would be sure to see that our mail delivery would continue. She was most helpful and reassuring. Mr. Benton did call back. He said that until that day, the Post Office had no idea that the railroad would be sending all the mail back.

Of course the Post Office didn't know who was or was not an employee of the Alaska Railroad. He mentioned having heard from several other people that morning as well, and asked me if I had any suggestions for alternate methods of delivery to our remote area. I suggested he contact one of the bush pilots flying out of Talkeetna and have the mail flown up to Gold Creek, the most central point for all of us, as well as having the only air strip in the area. Since none of us could get Post Office boxes, that was the only other thing we could come up with, besides having a mail man ride the train and throw off the mail at each place.

Mr. Benton said he would look into all possibilities and he asked me to call him back toward the end of the week. He assured me that no one's mail would be returned to the senders; it would all be held at the main Post Office at the airport until some other means of delivery was established.

Reassured that something was indeed being done, Clyde and I enjoyed the rest of Rondy week. Thursday morning I again called Mr. Benton. He said that air delivery would be possible, at a fraction of the cost, but we residents of the area would have to see that the air strip was maintained, and someone would have to be there to meet the mail plane each week. Meanwhile, he said, if we wished to come by the Post Office Friday, early in the afternoon, we could pick up everyone's mail and take it with us on the train when we went home Saturday, which we did. Quite a large and heavy sack of mail had accumulated over the week.

We received several letters from Senator Stevens explaining what he had done to assure our mail delivery. He also enclosed a letter from the Government Relations Department of the Post Office, to him, detailing the problem. The letter stated that "The Alaska Railroad's mail delivery service was unacceptable; since the Alaska Railroad was not able to provide better service, transportation of mail was converted to highway contract, except for the people living between Talkeetna and Hurricane along the railroad. The Alaska Railroad offered service to the families in this area at an approximate cost of $72,000 per year, a rate the postal service considered excessive.

It was a rather upsetting time for all of us along the tracks. It was an end to a very old tradition and an important part of our way of life.

***

Chapter 22 A New Era

And so a new era began, with the historic first in the small community of Gold Creek, at approximately 2:30 PM on Wednesday, February 22, 1984. The first mail plane, from K-2 Aviation, flew over our house, the pilot said "Howdy" to us on the C.B. radio, and continued on to the Gold Creek airstrip, six miles north. Our friends and neighbors Nancy Larson, and Mark and Linda Stadler, were all waiting at the air strip to meet the plane, and to put on a big sack of outgoing mail. They talked for a short time with the pilot, Jim Okonek, and with Mr. Benton, the Post Office supervisor, who flew up on the first mail run, and who was responsible for getting the mail plane to deliver our mail.

Our new mail service; a bush plane dropping off and picking up the mail... six miles from our homestead, once a week.

Everyone came to Gold Creek by snow machine or dogsled to pick up their mail. Someone would meet each mail plane, and we would all have to pick up our mail at Gold Creek any way we could. Depending on the time of year, we would travel by snow machine, skis, dog sled, or walk. In the summer some of us would have to go by boat, three wheeler, or walk, but one way or another we would get our mail. That first day though, Nancy had all sorts of food ready and we had a party at the section house.

It was fun and became another new tradition, not every week for sure, but often we would all get together. Nancy was such a wonderful cook, everyone gained weight at her parties, the pies, and other goodies she baked were legend.

She planned and put on Christmas parties, New Year parties, and there was even a wedding, when Nancy's youngest daughter, Jennifer, got married up there in Gold Creek. The only wedding ever held there. It was a fine beautiful sunny day in early June, and everything went off on schedule. The minister and his wife came, many other people not living along the tracks, came up by train. Some spent the night, others went back by train. The wedding was in the summertime when the passenger trains ran daily.

I went back to Wisconsin in late June 1984 to help my mother move back to California. She had been so crippled up with arthritis in the cold winter weather she wound up having to be hospitalized because she was in so much pain she couldn't walk. She decided to put her house up for sale and move back to California where it was much warmer. She called and asked me if I could help her get packed and moved when she sold her little house and I flew down there and began to pack for her. When we got everything sorted out that she decided to keep, we had a yard sale and a garage sale. Then I went and picked up a U-Haul trailer, hooked it to Mom's car, hired a couple of big burly strong men to help us load the trailer. They did such a good job; you could not have fitted a dime into that trailer, it was packed so tightly.

We took off the next day and drove to Laramie, Wyoming to see Shelley, Tim and Rachel. What a little doll she was!! It was sort of out of our way but Mom decided it was a good opportunity and not too much of a detour. The entire trip went well, I did all the driving. But when we got to the edge of Las Vegas, all of a sudden a fierce rain storm happened. The rain came down so heavily it was like being parked under a huge waterfall. We just happened to be near a casino, and so we parked in the parking lot and went inside. My mother loved to gamble. She would save her spare change all year in a glass jar so that whenever she got the chance, she could play the slot machines. She almost always won, or at least came out with what she started with.

She always gave her winnings to the church or orphanage she supported, and it was a lot of fun for me, watching her get as excited as a little kid, when she won. That time was no exception. She came out ahead by about $150. We made it just fine to California and unloaded the trailer and got Mom settled in with my brother John and his wife Donna and after resting for a day or two and visiting with everyone, I flew back home to Alaska.

The rest of that summer in Alaska was a long, rainy one, with very few days of sunshine. Bears were all over the woods and in the yard and the burn barrel, in the garden and eating the strawberries. One even came into the front porch, and when nothing was found to eat, it bit into a roll of paper towels, then left. Clyde fixed the front door so that it would latch, and also lock. That's one way to get the "honey-do" chores done! It probably would have helped to have a dog or two around to make noise. But we had none.

The fish were late that year, and it had rained so hard that all the creeks flooded and the Susitna River was up over the high water mark, in some places even up over the railroad tracks.

One morning I was the first one up. In my usual sluggish way I glanced out the front window and really woke up all at once. There was a very large brown grizzly digging in the garden very close to the house - what a thrill. We seldom saw grizzlies here, and that one was a beauty. He was obviously after some fish heads we had buried for organic fertilizer. We had done this many times before, when the salmon were all dying, without attracting any bears. I woke Clyde up, and very quietly we took pictures out the window, and then Clyde went out to the front porch and silently opened the door and took another picture.

As soon as the bear heard the camera click, he jerked up his head, turned tail and ran down the path to the tracks, turned south and was gone in a lot less time than this sentence took to write. He was about three years old, fat, sleek and about 600 pounds. Unfortunately, something was wrong with our camera and not a single picture turned out.

Chapter 23 Mom and I have our breaks

In June of 1985, my mom fell and broke her right ankle. Not to be outdone, in July of 1985, I fell and broke my left ankle, which meant I had to stay in town, where I was when I fell, for medical treatment and just sort of hibernated at Lisa's house. My good friend Nancy found out I was more or less housebound and she came to get me in her motor home, along with a neighbor from Gold Creek, Sharon McEuen. Nancy drove us to Denali National Park and we camped there. It was a very comfortable motor home. We also got a special pass, because I was handicapped which allowed us to drive way up into the Park, where the busses all go. At that time, none of the busses had handicapped access as there were no restrooms in them or wheelchair lifts. We had a wonderful time visiting and traveling through the Park. We saw lots of wild animals, more than we usually had in our yards, anyway. It was a great break from boredom. Denali National Park is a great place to play and it is bigger than the State of New Jersey.

When my mom got out of her cast, she flew up to see me, and while she was there, my cast came off. We both healed well and enjoyed Mom's stay. Once my cast was off, I could drive again and took Mom to several places including the homestead so she could see how much we had improved it since her last visit.

Two men from Germany came to Alaska to run Devil's Canyon Rapids. On a scale of one to ten, ten being the worst, Devil's Canyon rates about a fourteen, so they say. To the best of my knowledge, only one man has successfully run these rapids and lived to tell the tale. He even has a video of his adventure.

The German men did not make it. One of them grabbed a ledge and hoisted himself up onto it and the other one was bashed to death on the rocks and his boat was completely destroyed. These two men were a student and a teacher. The teacher was going to educate the student on how to run rapids. The teacher lost his helmet early on and he was the one that died. The student was the one that pulled himself onto the ledge and his boat was later found miles down the Susitna River.

My friend Nancy and her husband Harold were fishing at the confluence of the Susitna River and the mouth of Indian River when Nancy noticed an orange life jacket floating down the Susitna River. Harold jumped in his boat and ran it out to see if there was someone in the life jacket, and sure enough there was. Unfortunately he was dead. Harold could not get the man's body into the boat, so he fastened a rope to him and pulled him ashore. Then he ran the boat back to the section house and reported the incident to the authorities, who sent a helicopter up and then discovered the other man and rescued him from the ledge. The man who died turned out to be the teacher.

***

Clyde standing in the front yard on May 25th, 1991. It was an unusually late spring break up. The trees just behind Clyde to the right are in full spring leaf and brilliant green. We thought winter was never going to end!

Chapter 24 Friends Come To Call

Our good friends Edna and Elmer came again from Wisconsin to visit us and planned to spend a week on the homestead for Edna's R&R. Clyde and I went to Anchorage to meet their plane when it was time. We picked them up at the airport and on the way back to where we were all spending the night we saw a cow moose and her calf right beside the road. The cow was grazing and we stopped to take some pictures. Same thing happened three weeks later when they were leaving. On the way to the airport there was a huge bull moose with a marvelous set of antlers grazing on the grassy median and he posed beautifully for Elmer to take many pictures before we went on to the airport. The moral of this story is if you want to see a moose, go to Anchorage. They are very shy out here in the bush.

During the week they were with us on the homestead we had a grand show of black bear. At breakfast the first morning, one large fellow came sauntering up the railroad tracks and turned right in to continue up the path to our cabin, while we watched. The sun was shining and Elmer shot lots of film before the bear turned off and headed through the garden and into the woods.

A very large black bear stood up on his hind legs with his front paws on the piece of metal roofing nailed across the opening on the south side of the back porch. I heard the metal when it bent, and got to the window in time to see this large black bear saunter away toward the sawmill and the lumber drying shed. He kept going down the wood path, heading south, but he looked like the large blackie we saw from the train as we came home on Thursday.

One day I was sitting in the outhouse contemplating nature and enjoying the sun and scenery, all green and fluffy looking with here and there a little yellow and red just showing, when a great big black bear came out of the woods by the saw mill, walking towards me! Well, there I was, no gun, and so I yelled for Clyde, and he didn't hear me and so I beat on the side of the outhouse with my cane to make more noise and then the bear saw me and slowly turned around and went back the way he had come. I carefully came out and slowly walked home. They tell you not to run, no matter what, but in any case, I'm beyond running! I know God is watching over me and so I wasn't really worried - just a little excited??

***

May 25th, 1991. Clyde taking the snowmachine for what we are desperately hoping is the last spin of the winter. The trees behind Clyde are brilliant green, in full spring leaf; even with the ground still mostly covered in snow, the bursting forth of life will not be held back! Alaska continues to amaze us and fill us with wonder.

Chapter 25 Wedding Bells

In 1985 Debbie met Paul Bryner. They dated for a year and married on August 16, 1986. It was to be a church wedding, and Shelley, who was living in Iowa, was Debbie's matron of honor. We all got together and pooled resources and found a way. Shelley arrived with Rachel and Timmy the day before the wedding. Timmy was about sixteen months old. Nancy loaned us her motor home for the occasion, for the extra bodies to sleep in. The wedding was beautiful.

Shelley wanted to go to the homestead so badly that Bud planned a way to surprise her the next day. Actually the next day Debbie and Paul were going to catch the train and go spend a week of their honeymoon up at Sherman. Clyde and I had known that was the plan and before we left to come to town for the wedding, I painted two very large, four foot by eight foot pieces of plywood white and on one of them I painted a sign in bright red lettering that said "HONEYMOON IN PROGRESS" and the other one said, "TRESPASSERS WILL BE SHOT", with a little cupid and bow and arrow in one corner.

The sign says it all!.

Debbie and Paul got married on a Saturday. They stayed at the Hotel Captain Cook for their wedding night and planned to drive all the way up to Hurricane to catch the train down on Sunday afternoon. Meanwhile, Bud and Clyde and Shelley climbed into Bud's truck and they drove up to Talkeetna.

Shelley was thrilled to get to see that part of the country, but had no idea what Bud had arranged with his friend Jay Hudson of Hudson Air in Talkeetna. They got to a small lake where there was a plane on floats and Bud said, "Come on, you can see it from the air." The three of them climbed into Jay's floatplane, and flew up to Sherman.

The homestead from the air. The Susitna River is at the bottom of the picture, and the Alaska Railroad is the smoothly curving strip between the house and the river. The mouth of our creek is in the lower left corner of the picture. The airplane beached just off the left edge of the picture on a convenient sandbar.

Jay landed on the river and Shelley almost fainted with joy as they got out of the plane. Jay took off again, and the three of them hiked through the woods and across the tracks and up the path to home. Bud and Clyde propped up the signs in the front yard so they could be seen by every passing train and Shelley took a short nap after exploring and looking and being home. Shortly thereafter the Southbound train came with Debbie and Paul on it. Bud, Clyde and Shelley were waiting and they all hugged Deb and Paul as they got off, and then got on the train for the ride back to Talkeetna. The signs were a big hit, evidently, because Deb said later that every train that went by slowed way down so the tourists could take pictures, at least twice a day. So the signs were a hit with the tourists. Meanwhile, I stayed in town and babysat my two adorable grandchildren and had a great time. A few days later, Shelley and babies went back to Laramie.

Paul is an insurance underwriter, and he has done very well. Debbie works for several Internet companies. She is also a Pampered Chef Consultant. They have two beautiful children, a girl and a boy. Kate was born in 1988 and Rhys in 1992. Kate has graduated from high school and Rhys will graduate in 2011. They live in South Anchorage.

My mother and brother Paul came from California, and Clyde's mom and sister came from Missouri for the wedding. Edna and Elmer were there as well, from Wisconsin.

Lisa, meanwhile, had met and dated an Army man, Forest Taylor. Guess it must have been catching, because they decided to get married also just a few months later. Theirs was not a church wedding. They got married in a greenhouse, full of flowers and green plants and it was very beautiful. It was snowy outside so the greenhouse idea worked out very well. Everyone wanted them to have a double wedding with Debbie and Paul because nobody could afford two trips to Alaska. But it was not meant to be. And Forest and Lisa did not want a big wedding.

A few months later, Forest was transferred to Charleston, South Carolina by the Army and so they went. Lisa was most unhappy. It was not a good move for her. But she made the best of it, and they got on with their lives. Lisa wrote that the wages were so low in the area, and she said she must be spoiled, because at that time they had nothing like the stores we had up here. If she wanted to buy meat, she had to go to a meat market. If she wanted to buy drugs, (aspirin or prescription drugs) she had to go to a drug store. If she wanted to buy fish she had to go to a fish market. She said it took her all day to do a week worth of shopping.

They were living near Charleston when Hurricane Hugo blew into the Gulf Coast. Lisa said she was so frightened she hardly knew what to do. Part of their roof blew off, and she said they were lucky it wasn't worse. But they had to move out and found a house to share with another couple farther away from town.

Eventually they split up, having decided their marriage was a mistake, and Lisa came back home. Later, she met Eugene Larmi, and she was sure he was the 'one'. We had bought a little house in Anchorage by that time, and when Lisa and Gene set a date for their wedding it was held in the backyard of our house, under a huge red and white striped tent on a beautiful day in summer with lots of folks attending. A Lutheran minister officiated, and several months later Lisa and Gene started attending that church. They have become quite active church members over the years.

They have a beautiful daughter, MaryAlice. She will graduate high school in another year and plans to go on to college. They all grow up so fast!! They live in East Anchorage. Gene is a computer programmer and Lisa is a Human Resources professional.

We have thirteen grandchildren: six boys, seven girls. The picture of all the grandkids is the first one in the picture section at the end of this book. It was taken at one of our birthday parties, and probably the only time we could get all 13 of them in one place long enough to take a picture. It has become a tradition in our family, started by our kids, to put on a big party for us in a park. Our birthdays are both on June 17th, and our wedding anniversary as well, and every few years, Father's day happens on or near the same date. Also Lisa's birthday is only five days difference, June 22nd. They put on a big barbecue and invite all our and their friends and we have an enjoyable day. It has seldom rained, but when it did one time, we were all under a pavilion roof anyway, and it was pleasant.

***

Three of the Finley children. Left to right: Rachel (the oldest), Greg (the youngest), and Danny. Sitting on a rock near their Eagle River home with the family dog, Fawn

Chapter 26 Devastating Loss

It was February 1988, ten degrees below zero, with a slight wind blowing, enough to make it miserable. Clyde and I were out by the tracks skinning a moose the train had hit, about half mile south of our house when along came the Gold Creek section foreman to tell us that there was an urgent phone call for us at the section house. He said we needed to call the party back right away. So we hopped on the gas car and rode up to Gold Creek and called the number and it was my brother Paul. He said we needed to come right away to California if we wanted to see my sister Beth, that she was in the hospital dying and they held out no hope at all for her. She had pneumonia and she also had no immune system left after fighting to get rid of her non-Hodgkin's Lymphoma for the past two years.

We said we would do what we could and would call him back when we had made our arrangements. I called Lisa and asked her to do whatever she had to get tickets for us by midnight at the soonest, and called Debbie and asked if she or Paul could drive up to Hurricane and pick us up, since it was a train day and we would be catching the train around 1:30 or 2:00 PM. That meant they would have to leave right away from Anchorage to get there in time. She said, "No problem". The section foreman drove us back home, and we hurriedly finished skinning the meat and packed it home, hung it up in the shed, put away the machinery, packed a suit case and made it out to the tracks just as the northbound train was coming. The section foreman had called the dispatcher and told him to inform the train conductor that we would be catching the train for an emergency trip.

When we got to Hurricane, the wind was blowing harder and it was probably colder than 10 below, at least it felt like it. Deb and Paul were not there, and no one was home at the section house there either. But we only had to wait and stomp our feet to try to keep warm for about

10 minutes before they arrived. We piled into the car, baggage and all and they turned around and drove back to Anchorage. Clyde and I only had time to hurriedly take a shower, change into clean clothes and get to the airport to catch the midnight 'red eye' flight.

We arrived in Los Angeles at 9:00 AM and were met by my mother and brother Paul and hurried to the hospital. Beth was still with us, but not for long. She was glad to see us. We were the last of her family to arrive. My poor baby sister was burning up with fever, scared, she knew she was dying and what a hopeless helpless feeling, not being able to help or change anything. Her temperature was 108 degrees. Nothing was working for her. The antibiotics, the oxygen, ice packs, nothing. She was only 46 years old.

We all joined hands and made a circle around her bed and said the Lord's Prayer. Slowly and quietly she slipped away and was gone.

Our poor mother was so …well you can imagine how she was. We all were. My three brothers, my youngest sister Kathy and Clyde and I were stunned with disbelief. We were so certain she would come around and recover. It was unthinkable.

We felt we had to stay on and be near the rest of our family for awhile. All of us felt the same. We made the arrangements for funeral and so forth, and packed up Beth's house and helped in any way we could taking turns being with our mother to make sure she was okay. Brother John had just finished building a couple of new homes and we helped him landscape the yards. We all kept busy and tried to cope.

The stress of the funeral and all the sadness was overwhelming for everyone. Beth's boss, Katy Bishop offered us a weekend at her "cabin" in Big Bear to escape it all. So my sister Kathy and our close friend and sister in our hearts, Cheryl Heimer and myself all took off for Big Bear with the keys to Katy's place. When we arrived we were all astounded at what Katy called a "cabin". It was a fabulous two story house, beautifully furnished inside with panoramic views from every window. Big pine tree forest all around. We spent our time walking in the woods, meditating and praying about recent events, bonding with each other after a long absence and mostly trying to shake off the unbearable sadness we all felt.

It was a renewal of our spirits and a wonderful weekend in spite of everything. I was able to connect with my sister Kathy like never before. When I left home to get married, she was only four years old, so we never had a chance to really get to know each other as sisters should. Since that weekend in Big Bear we continue to nurture a close relationship that remains strong to this day. We left some Easter lilies on the table for Katy and she told us the whole house smelled just heavenly the next time she came up.

When we finally went back home to Alaska, we realized we were not going to make it financially unless we went to work for awhile. Living on retirement really wasn't getting us anywhere financially. In fact we were going in the hole a little deeper each month. We had a family conference and decided to spend, at least for a short while, more time in Anchorage were there was work. I went to work for a temporary agency, and eventually ran that agency. Clyde worked on building or remodeling projects with Bud when he had enough work. We stayed with Lisa for awhile, and then moved on to Debbie's.

Bud and Diane had moved to Maui, Hawaii where Bud was hired to supervise a job, which lasted for two years. We always went home to Sherman to spend as much time as possible there.

***

Chapter 27 Clyde's Dream Comes True

Clyde finally got his boat. A thirty-three foot long, twenty foot wide Trimaran hull, with sails, motor, unfinished inside, needed a mast and fittings. It was in a barn in Wasilla, and needed to be moved to Anchorage, where Clyde could work on it when he wasn't working to pay for it.

Clyde motoring the Arctic Tern on a calm day on Cook Inlet, near Anchorage.

It needed paint, inside and out. We found out we could move it with a permit only between 2 AM and 5 AM on a given date, with an escort vehicle in front and one in back. So we got together a crew of our kids and us, and rented a big truck and flatbed trailer and jacked up the hull and somehow got it on the flatbed trailer and cinched it down tightly, moved it all the way to Anchorage. It took up a lane and a half and I was amazed at how people ignored the signs of WIDE LOAD plastered all over the lead and following car and just kept driving.

At that time there was only a two lane highway from Wasilla to Anchorage, with one lane going north and one lane going south. It was a hairy trip indeed, but we made it in about 3 ½ hours. Then we parked the boat down by the inlet. That was before there was a ramp or any type of accommodation built there. Therefore, we did not have to pay space rent. Other folks had their boats there also, and had had no problems with vandalism or theft.

When Clyde was not working, he put in time fixing up the boat. I meanwhile had started a job with the Attorney Generals' office downtown, a temporary job, supposed to last three months, but actually it lasted for seven. We rented a small apartment, so we wouldn't have to keep moving around from kid to kid, and dug in for the duration.

By the end of that year, we figured out we should be buying a house, at least then we could sell it and get some of our money back, instead of throwing it away on rent. We began looking, and finally found a small two bedroom house, only 760 square feet, but larger than the apartment we were in, and larger on the inside than it looked. The payments were only about $25 more than we were paying for rent, so we took it.

That year Clyde's mom came up to spend the summer with us. Bud and Diane had been living for the last two years in Maui, Hawaii, and had another child, their third. Bud's job was finished and they were moving back to Alaska. At the same time, Shelley, Tim and their 4.5 children, (one on the way) had decided finally to relocate to Alaska. We met Bud and Diane at the airport with their baby, Amanda. Diane was pregnant with the fourth child, Vanessa.

Our house was so small that Clyde's mom stayed with Debbie and Paul at their house, which was about five blocks away. The house was full to bursting. Bud and his family had our bedroom. We put up a crib for the baby and the other two kids, Jackie and Nathan, slept on pallets on the carpeted floor.

Meanwhile I cleared out the second bedroom, which had been my home office, and soon thereafter Shelley, Tim and their four kids arrived. There was no housing available at that time as things were pretty tight. At night, Clyde and I went over to Debbie and Paul's house to sleep which left a little room in our living room for anyone who needed to spread out. It was three weeks before anyone found a place to rent, and that was Bud and his family.

That gave Shelley and her family a little more room. Soon they, too found a place to rent and moved out and we moved back home once again. Oh, we were home every day, after work, and every night we got to spend with Clyde's mom over at Debbie and Paul's house. Soon we went back home to the homestead for several weeks, so Clyde's mom could have some R&R. That was some hectic summer. But we were so happy all our kids were home once more.

All boat owners were notified we had to move our boats from where they were parked, because work was going to start to build a large cement ramp and boatyard and so we moved the boat. We had to hire a crane to do it and they put it in the water after stepping the mast. Clyde anchored it out there so it was okay except when the tide went out; then it was stuck in the mud until the tide came back in.

Clyde arranged with son-in-law Tim to help him sail it to Homer or some other place where we could put it for the winter, since Anchorage was not an ice free harbor. They set off one day, and only made it as far as Nikiski where they finally gave up. It was so rough, and the wind in the wrong direction, they had to motor all the way, and the motor was a small one so it took forever to go a mile. So they turned around and came back. They could sail all the way back, and it was so much faster. It was Tim's first time on a boat and he was disenchanted with the whole thing. His comment was, "Well, it was an experience."

We had the boat taken out of the water and parked on a cradle inside a chain link fence by the boat ramp where we had to pay $50 a month to store it for the winter, in Anchorage.

The following summer, Bud went with Clyde and they sailed and motored all the way to Homer and had it parked in a slip there for 'only' $150 a month. Clyde decided that trip that he was too old for that sort of thing; it was too hard on his back, etc., so he put the boat up for sale. We did drive down to Homer and putter around on the boat sometimes and sail it around Resurrection Bay. It would really go, but I had no desire to take it out on the open ocean, and neither, I think, did Clyde.

***

Chapter 28 Freak Accident

I was in a freak accident, was at the airport at midnight picking up some friends, when the van behind my car ran into me. I had been loading luggage into my trunk and just happened to look up as the van crushed my right knee between the two bumpers. It was September, raining, dark and by the time the man got back in his van and put the thing into reverse to back off me, it felt like the bones in and around my knee were smashed. The airport attendant wanted me to lie down, but I refused. It was raining, the pavement was soaking wet, I couldn't move without excruciating pain, and just sat on my bumper with the trunk lid open and waited for the ambulance to come.

They put me on a stretcher and took me to the hospital, called my daughter Shelley, who was a nurse. The x-rays showed no broken bones, boy was I surprised. Some how they got me in a wheel chair and Shelley took me home. It took four months for the swelling to go down enough for a doctor to do arthroscopic surgery and clean up the mess of torn ligaments, displaced pieces of cartilage, and mashed muscle, and so on. It hurt worse than ever after that, for awhile, but eventually felt better and I decided I'd had enough of town. Clyde had as well, by then. So we put our house in Anchorage up for sale, and moved *home* to Sherman. And there we are to this day. We have had many bears visit, a few marten, fox, porcupine and ermine.

***

Chapter 29 Andre, the Family 'Watch' Cat

One night, when Andre the cat was there with us, it had been raining for days and I thought she was just having a fit because she hates the rain and hadn't been out of the house for days. Anyway, I heard this Thump! Downstairs - I had been nearly asleep, and I got up to see what the noise was all about. There was Andre on the steps looking out the back window all excited, her fur standing up all over, and I looked out too but saw nothing. So I thought that she had just jumped either on, or off the rocking chair causing it to bang against the closet doors downstairs and I went back to bed.

It was in early July so it was still light outside. In the morning Clyde found a pile of bear scat by the woodshed and the burn barrel was knocked over, and also he found a piece of exterior siding ripped off the house just below the south window in the living room. I had neglected to shut the curtains downstairs, and evidently the bear was looking in and must have seen Andre. Also there were muddy bear paw prints on the big picture window.

We had Andre the cat with us periodically. This time it was winter. She had caught two or three mice in the house that I knew of, all shrews, and chased a marten out of the house or helped, at least. That darn thing got in again last Tuesday and it took Clyde and I two whole hours to get it out again. It ran upstairs and hid behind and under the low three drawer chest in the corner behind the sewing machine, and growled at us.

Every time it ran under the day bed in the living room where Andre was hiding, she hissed and growled at it and chased it back out again. I guess we had relaxed and forgot to check and bolt the back door. But meanwhile it had been so cold that Andre would not go outside, and just threw fits in the house.

The marten got in to eat the rest of the chicken meat that I forgot about in a pan on the top of the wood cook stove and left bones all over the top of the stove. When Clyde opened the door so it could go out, it just growled at him and ran the other way. It didn't get to finish the meat, though. The birds got the rest of it.

But we kept opening windows and doors and trying to get it out, and it kept running the other way. It was minus 20 that morning. So after it left, finally we had to clean that corner of the upstairs all over again. It was almost as cold inside as it was outside by that time.

Yes, we never had a dull life, though I would have liked to try dull sometime for a change. We got home from town the last time only to find the creek had dried up and we had no source of water. Luckily Clyde had filled up everything before we left for town, so we had drinking water at least for a week or so, but then it rained for two days and nights, and everything, including our creek flooded.

Sections of the railroad tracks washed out in six or seven places and buried our new water pump under a foot of water. Huge rocks and trees were coming down the creek, and we were fortunate that the water pump hadn't been washed away. Clyde took it apart and discovered that it was full of sand and grit. He cleaned it all out and I convinced him to box up all the parts and bring it to town, as soon as the train was able to run again, and we took it to a small engine shop and the guy put it all back together for $25 – including a new gasket and spark plug.

We saw a big rangy beautiful wolf walk down the tracks two days ago. He was so light gray he was almost white.

***

Chapter 30 Strange Accidents

On May 31, 2003 Bud and Cynthia were at Sherman to spend the weekend with us. Clyde had just obtained his new chain saw mill and was outside cutting boards out of a tree trunk. The rest of us were in the kitchen when Clyde came hobbling in holding onto his leg, which was bleeding through the shredded cloth of his pants, just above his knee.

"What happened?" we all asked and he replied "The mill broke and shoved the chain saw down onto my leg." We got him into a chair, and Bud cut off the pants leg to see about the damage. It was a terrible looking cut, like hamburger, all ground up in a line about an inch wide and at least an inch deep, and clear across his leg just above the knee and bleeding profusely. Cynthia said she couldn't look, and so stayed over by the sink.

Bud got some sterile pads and put pressure on the cut while Cynthia got some water and antiseptic from the medicine cabinet and I got on the CB radio to call Hardin, our neighbor up north. Clyde was not feeling any pain at the moment, and was worried about bleeding all over the carpet, and also about his chain saw which was still running full speed outside by the log he had been working on. I ran out and shut the chain saw down and continued to call Hardin on the CB.

Hardin finally answered the CB, but he was all the way up at Chulitna and did not have a radio phone, but when I told him what had happened, he ran to his nearest neighbor to use his radio phone. He talked to the emergency rescue service and they wanted to know about the bleeding. Hardin called me back on the CB and I told him it was bleeding steadily, but not spurting. So they considered it not a life threatening emergency since there were no arteries involved.

But it was enough of an emergency to justify sending someone out to get him. He is diabetic and it would be really bad if he went into shock, they said. The railroad came through yet again and sent a truck up with a back seat to pick him up. They put him on a stretcher and loaded him into the back seat.

Meanwhile, Bud had more or less stopped the bleeding, and splinted the leg so Clyde couldn't bend it. There was an ambulance waiting at Hurricane, where the tracks cross the road, and they put Clyde in the ambulance. By that time, he was beginning to feel the pain. It looked to us like he might have cut a tendon. But when he got to the hospital, the doctor who stitched him up said it was only the muscle sheath and that Clyde had been very lucky not to have hit the artery, less than an inch away from the cut.

Bud, Cynthia and I caught the southbound train and got off at Talkeetna. I drove right to the hospital and they had just finished stitching Clyde up and signed him out to go home. That sort of put a damper on the whole summer for Clyde, but he healed up very well, and there is hardly any scar there now.

***

Another strange thing happened to us in the summer of 2006. For some reason the salmon run was late getting up our way; once the salmon arrived, it rained so hard all the creeks flooded and washed some of the railroad tracks out. We were on the little train on Friday, because I was scheduled to do a book signing on Saturday, noon to 4:00 PM at Talkeetna Gifts & Collectibles.

My first book had just been published and the book signing was my very first. It was very successful, since it had been announced on Talkeetna radio station, and we put signs out all over the place. It was a lot of fun, too. We met a lot of people we hadn't seen for some time, and it was sort of an "old home week" for us.

One of the old acquaintances we had not seen for a long time was Dave, also known as "Dirty Dave" Gonzales, 'Dirt' for short. Years before, he would always stop at our house on his way north with his dog team. He would come in to get warm and we would visit awhile, feed him coffee and cookies or cinnamon rolls or whatever we had going and he would go on once he was warm. He was quite entertaining, and the kids really liked him and he was always nice and polite, would joke with the kids and catch up on the news.

But back to Friday's train - we were very late, and about Mile 247 we had to stop and wait for an hour and a half for a bulldozer to come and clear a landslide off the tracks, which happened in front of the big tourist train. We were parked about a block behind the big train. The conductor and engineer ran out of time on the big train while we were parked there, and so our conductor and engineer, still having plenty of time left, moved our train up to the big one and fastened us to the back of it, and they got on the big train.

Right after that, a huge hunk of mountain with rocks and trees and mud came down on the tracks right where we had been parked! The tourists that were on our train were all upset, with good reason. Five more minutes and we would all have been in the river, which was right up to within inches of the tracks. I hope we have not used up all our guardian angels, but I know we have kept them very busy!

The trains did not run for three days, and they had to send a helicopter to rescue a man who was an insulin dependent diabetic from the cabin by Sherman siding, one mile south of our house, along with his niece. The rest of them had to wait until a special train, (ours) could rescue them and get them out, which was Monday, three days later. They sent a special train slowly just to rescue anyone who was stranded. The railroad always manages to fix things as rapidly as possible.

Last summer, 2009, one of the passengers on the Denali Express train had a heart attack. The train was close to our place, and they backed up to be right here when the helicopter they had called arrived. Ours was the perfect place to land, close to the tracks, minimum of trees and brush. They landed successfully and got the unconscious lady out and treated her and took her away. We learned later that she was just fine, having gotten the prompt treatment she needed had saved her life.

During the summer we park our little motor home in Talkeetna, and catch the train in on Saturday afternoon, spend the night, go to church on Sunday morning and catch the train back home at noon. It works out very well. But in winter the trains run in the wrong direction to make it to church on Sundays so we don't get to go very often; only if we are in town for more than a week.

Summer, 2009. The emergency medivac helicopter landing in our front yard to evacuate a heart attack victim from the passenger train.

My friend Nancy lives in Talkeetna now, since the railroad did away with the section house at Gold Creek, and she runs a wonderful bed and breakfast place. One summer we parked all summer on her lot. For the last few years we have parked in the parking lot of the Catholic church, which is very near the depot. That has worked out very well.

During the winters we park the motor home in Bud and Cynthia's driveway in Wasilla, and if the weather is not too horrifically cold, we sleep there, in our little motor home. Otherwise, we drive into Anchorage and sleep in our bedroom at Lisa and Gene's home. Bud likes to tell people he makes his parents sleep in his driveway.

We had a wonderful time with Edna and Elmer during their next time in Alaska.. We went to Cordova on the new and very fast ferry from Whittier, and spent three days there camping, each couple in their own little camper. We saw the most astounding glacier, the Childs Glacier, more than twenty stories tall and just across the Copper River. It calved all the time making huge booms, bangs and crashes, echoing in the canyon behind. It was astounding. We had great fellowship and a marvelous visit while there. We left there and we all went to Sherman and had a full week of sweet relaxation together.

Now we have reached the winter of our lives, and of course, don't know how long we still have to live on this earth. We've had a good life with plenty of adventures and have been blessed with wonderful children,

Clyde and Mary relaxing in Bud and Cynthia's home in Wasilla.

grandchildren, and a great grandchild. If it is God's will, we may travel a bit and enjoy other sights and sounds, and live as long as we are able at our home in our beloved valley at Sherman. Life has been interesting, to say the least, and we're thankful we have been so blessed.

***

Epilog

Excerpts from travel diary: 2006

We decided to snowbird it this year. We flew down to Las Vegas on October 10th, stayed at a "weekly" apartment/hotel and during that week, looked around for a motor home and bought it. Soon it needed a lot of work. t was a 1988 Bounder, 27 feet long, with all the bells and whistles - a lot different than our little 18 footer.

We had a nice time at the RV park in Pahrump, Nevada when we found that there were vacancies for both Sunday and Monday nights, and so there we were at this lovely place. There were pine trees and other trees, green grass, many ducks on the lake, an aerated fountain in the middle of the lagoon, and large enough spaces that we could put our awning up and sit outside in the cool breeze and enjoy the view and the sun.

Camping out in BLM lands in Arizona was quite nice. No charge and we had 14 days of camping if we wanted to use it. Also when we come back we do not need a permit for two or three days of camping. While at camp, we made a fire behind the motor home, we heard a coyote yipping and turned to see him looking at us through some brush nearby. He circled our area and then went away. He was pretty.

Talked to the kids yesterday and Saturday, and talked to brother John today and we will be seeing him December 27th in Vegas. Also we will be going to meet granddaughter Jackie at her husband's grandparents, John and Faye's home in Victorville on December 26th, if all goes well. Brother John and Donna going to China in February. Brother Paul and Mary are home from the Bahamas and doing well.

Talked to my friend Margie Mullins today and things are just about the same there in Delta Junction, Alaska - cold. It had been 35° below zero last time I talked with her and her pipes were all frozen. Then it got to 60 below and well, now she said, it was up to zero, and pipes were okay. It has been in the 60's here and the 40's at night. Seems cold to me! We miss all the kids so much, but we will be home for Easter, God willing.

Spent three days in Yuma, Arizona, visited with Doug and Geri. Doug is Edna's brother. Such nice people they are. Will be looking forward to seeing them around the end of January again when Edna and Elmer are there. Had extensive work done on the motor home, put in a new flywheel and starter, also three U bolts and four belts. The bill was $1,367. Drives much better now and starts every time.

We parked in Lizard Lane motor home park in Quartzsite, Arizona and will be leaving for Parker on the way up to Vegas. We will be able to see Parker in daylight this time. Should be pretty!

Heard it snowed on the mountains all around where David and Jennifer, my sister Kathy's son and daughter-in-law live and is cold there. We plan to park for a day or so in Henderson, Nevada.

We spent a nice Christmas with David, Jennifer, Cindy and Kathy, Daniel and the kids, also Jennifer's mother April, a very nice lady, and another new friend. David and Jennifer gave us a Buick automobile for Christmas. It is now January 4th, and David and Clyde are working on the car trying to get it to run. I have sent off for license and insurance for it so hope it runs, at least. It is still cold and windy here and we may be moving on soon, I hope. David fixed a great dinner and we all enjoyed the day totally.

We need to be in Yuma by end of January at least and then over to my brother Paul's house in Ramona, California for boxes. Hopefully Kathy will be all finished with her hyperbaric treatments by then and can join us there. Jackie and Jeremy want to come to Paul's while we are there.

We thoroughly enjoyed seeing them both and Jeremy's mom and dad and grandparents when we went to Victorville December 27th We had such a great visit, and great food and fellowship and spent the night in our motor home in their driveway. God is good.

We got nothing else done in the way of traveling, only went to Quartzsite, and Yuma. Decided not to go to the Phoenix area, nor even in Tucson or Bob's folks in Black Canyon City or Cheryl and Jim in Sedona. We didn't get to go see Lisa B in Utah. Wanted to go to Organ Pipe and several other state or national park places people told us about in Arizona, but wound up spending weeks in the desert and doing nothing but spending money. Going three times a week to Mexico for weeks on end for chelation treatments for Clyde and enjoying the sun.

Went to Paul's for a weekend and the weather was fine. We met Kathy and Cindy and the next day started working on the storage garage Kathy had been paying on for seven years. Unpacking boxes and dresser drawers and throwing away whatever could be and giving away what could not be thrown away.

When we are finished with all that, and there is a lot of it, we will go back to Las Vegas once again, unpack all Kathy's stuff and pack all our stuff and finally get to go back home to Alaska. On the way back to Vegas our car overheated and burnt up on Baker grade, which is a 16 mile long uphill grade. We had it towed back to Baker after unloading all the boxes of stuff and loading them into the motor home. I must say though, the motor home didn't even overheat. We tried to donate the car to charity –and they would not take it. But it was useful for almost three months.

The bright spot of this whole trip was the week or so spent at Doug and Geri's house and visiting with all of them and Edna's birthday party. It was super, with her two brothers and her sister and all their spouses attending.

Each weekend I got to call my kids and talk to them, and that eased my loneliness somewhat but also it made me miss them all more. I don't know if I can do this again. It is really not my thing. Short term motor home living is alright, but not for five and a half long seemingly endless months! We put our motor home in storage and flew home.

We left Anchorage to fly to Nevada to be snowbirds for the second year in a row on November 26, 2007. Gas was terribly expensive and we spent most of the four months there in the cancer treatment center of Nevada at one doctor or another getting treatment for Clyde who was diagnosed with cancer just before we left Alaska.

His doctor in Alaska said he would do nothing because of Clyde's age. His exact words were, "Yeah, you have cancer." We said, "What are you going to do to get rid of it?" The doctor said, "Nothing, Something else will kill you first, so live with it."

We disagreed, and went on to Las Vegas and to the Cancer Center of Nevada where Clyde received treatment so he would not have to "live with it" and it is now two years later and Clyde is fine, cancer all gone, feeling like a new man at 81. All the previous problems with joint pain and such have also gone away. I'm not a medical person, but I wonder if all that was connected?

We did not go outside last winter at all nor this winter, of 2010, and it was great being at home all winter. We had many people for company, not all at once this last summer, but most of the summer was taken up with company at the homestead and with book signings, mostly at the Denali Park bookstore, and the Princess train and at the last Moose Dropping Festival in Talkeetna. I am so sorry the townspeople canceled that tradition.

We decided that snow birding was really not for us. We miss our kids and grandkids too much and also Alaska and our homestead. At some point, though, we will have to go back for a short while anyway, to see about selling our motor home. It's a nice one, about the right size but way too expensive to run around in, at least for us.

As we can, we plan to make short trips as we used to, to keep in touch with family and friends down south and grandkids and our great grandson, if we are able. We would love to go to Ireland. We planned to go for our 55th wedding anniversary, but other commitments came up and we weren't able to. Perhaps for our 56th, coming up in June, 2010.

We met a priest from Ireland and he invited us to stay at the monastery, which is housed in an old castle in the south near Limerick, Ireland. Sounds exciting to us and we are looking forward to it. My grandmother (my father's mother) was Irish.

***

All the LIFE we lived here. God has richly blessed us!

Appendix A

Homestead Recipes – Sherman City Hall Specialties

CINNABARB PIE

Make two 8 or 9 inch pie shells, bake. (Or buy 2 graham cracker crust pie shells.)

Put in a medium pan and heat:

1 quart cooked rhubarb

1 ½ cups sugar, (or to taste)

½ cube butter or margarine

1 teaspoon lemon juice (optional)

Separate 6 eggs. Put the yolks into a medium bowl. Put the whites into a bowl and refrigerate until later. (These will make the meringue.)

In a bowl, mix together:

6 egg yolks

1 can evaporated milk

6 tablespoons corn starch

Mix well, until smooth

ADD TO HEATED MIXTURE ABOVE. Cook until thick, stirring constantly to prevent   scorching. Add red food color, a few drops at a time until pink, or salmon colored.

REMOVE FROM HEAT AND COOL COMPLETELY (Must be totally cool or will melt the meringue and be a real mess)

Fill the baked pie shells with the rhubarb custard mixture, once cooled.

When filling is completely cool, take out the six egg whites and beat until stiff peaks form. Then slowly add 6 tablespoons sugar, beating all the while, and one tablespoon cinnamon and continue beating until shiny. Put filling into pie shells, either baked shells or graham cracker crust shells. Add meringue on top and bake in a preheated very hot oven, 500 degrees or more for two to five minutes watching constantly so it does not burn. Makes two 9 inch pies. (You can halve the recipe to make only one pie.) Best served chilled.

Even people who do not like rhubarb usually love this pie. It is creamy, smooth, tart, sweet and delicious.

RHUBARB CUSTARD PIE

4 cups diced rhubarb, (about 1 ½ pounds)

1 unbaked 9 inch pie shell

3 eggs 3 tablespoons milk

1 ½ cups sugar

¼ cup flour

1/8 teaspoon fresh grated nutmeg

½ tablespoon butter

Place rhubarb in pie shell. In a small bowl, beat together eggs, milk, sugar, flour and nutmeg until smooth. Pour over rhubarb, smoothing evenly. Cut butter into small pieces and dot top of pie with butter. Place pie in a preheated, 400 degree oven and bake for 20 minutes.

Reduce heat to 350 degrees and bake 20 minutes longer or until filling is set. Cool to room temperature before cutting. Makes one pie.

CABBAGE AND SPARERIB SOUP

1 tsp caraway seeds

1 tsp paprika

2 tsp dry mustard

1 tbsp brown sugar

Salt

Pinch of cayenne pepper

1 ¼ lbs pork spareribs, (about 8 ribs or ½ rack)

1 head garlic, peeled, cloves crushed

Vegetable spray

6 cups rich chicken stock

2 cups diced yellow onions

6 generous cups green cabbage in 1 inch dice

½ tsp freshly ground black pepper

2 tsp chopped parsley for garnish

In a spice grinder process caraway seeds, paprika and mustard until fine. Turn into a bowl with brown sugar, 1 tsp salt and the cayenne, fluff with fingertips.

Dry ribs well with paper towels, and rub both sides with spices and crushed garlic. Place ribs on a small rack or plate, cover with plastic wrap and refrigerate at least 6 hours or overnight.

Adjust oven rack to lowest position, and heat oven to 425 degrees. Spray a sheet pan with vegetable spray. Brush garlic cloves from ribs, place ribs in the sheet pan and roast until a deep golden brown, about 30 minutes.. Remove from oven.

Transfer ribs to a 6 quart Dutch oven; pour rendered fat, (about 2 tbsps) from sheet pan into a large heavy skillet, and set aside. Place sheet pan on 2 burners over high heat, add 1 cup water and stir with a wooden spoon to dislodge browned bits. Pour deglazing liquid and stock into Dutch oven, cover and bring to simmer over medium high heat. Reduce heat to low, and simmer gently until ribs are tender, turning occasionally, about 1 ½ hours. Remove ribs from broth and cool slightly.

While ribs simmer, sauté onions and cabbage in skillet over medium high heat, stirring frequently, until lightly browned, about 20 minutes. Add 1 tsp salt and the black pepper; stir to combine. Set aside.

Pull pork off bones, trim off bits of cartilage and dice meat. Discard bones. Return meat to soup base, add cabbage and onions and simmer about 15 minutes. Serve garnished with parsley.

CABBAGE AND POTATO GRATIN WITH MUSTARD BREAD CRUMBS

1/3 cup slab bacon in ¼ inch dice

¾ cup yellow onion in ¼ inch dice

1 ½ cups yukon gold potatoes in ½ inch dice

1 small bay leaf

1 ¼ tsp salt

½ tsp freshly ground black pepper

8 cups green cabbage in 1 inch dice

½ cup heavy cream

FOR THE BREAD CRUMBS:

2 tbsps unsalted butter

1 ¼ cups fresh white bread crumbs

1 garlic clove, minced

Pinch salt

Pinch cayenne pepper

2 tsp Dijon mustard

2 tsp chopped parsley

¾ cup comte or gruyere cheese, grated

Heat oven to 425 degrees. Place bacon in a 12 inch sauté pan over medium heat and cook about 2 minutes. Add onion and sauté, stirring frequently, until bacon is crisp and onion is golden, about 5 minutes. Add potatoes, bay leaf, salt and pepper and sauté, stirring, for 2 minutes. Add cabbage and sauté, stirring frequently until cabbage wilts a bit, about 5 minutes.

Turn cabbage mixture into a shallow 1 ½ or 2 quart casserole dish. Pour cream into sauté pan and reduce over high heat, stirring constantly with a wooden spoon until cream is reduced by half, about 2 minutes. Pour cream over cabbage and stir to mix. Cover casserole with foil. Bake 10 minutes.

Meanwhile, melt butter in a 10 inch skillet over low heat. When it is foamy, add bread crumbs and sauté, stirring constantly with a wooden spoon until crisp and golden, 5 to 7 minutes. Remove from heat, add garlic, salt, cayenne pepper, mustard and parsley, stirring well to combine. Sprinkle casserole with cheese, then with bread crumbs and return to oven uncovered. Bake until fragrant and bubbling slightly around edges, about 5 minutes. Serve as a side dish to roast fowl, pork or meaty fish like halibut.

BASIC BREAD RECIPE

Put in a large bowl:

1 quart hot (not boiling) water

1 tablespoon salt

2 tablespoons sugar

1/3 to ½ cup oil, OR ½ cup solid shortening or butter or margarine.

Stir well.

Meanwhile, in a small bowl, put ½ to ¾ cup very warm water, add 1 tablespoon sugar and stir well. Make sure water is very warm but not hot. Add two tablespoons yeast, or 2 packages and stir until mixed and set aside to see if it bubbles. (about 5 minutes) If it does not foam or bubble, perhaps the yeast is no good, or the water too warm or cold. Try again with the yeast.

To the first mixture, add 2 cups flour, 1 cup at a time, mixing after each addition. When the yeast mixture has bubbled, stir it well and add it to the flour mixture and stir well. Keep adding flour, a cup at a time, until the dough is stiff enough to knead. Then turn out on well floured surface and knead well, for 10 to 20 minutes until light, elastic and smooth. Grease or oil the bowl and put the dough back into the bowl, coating each surface with oil. Cover with a clean towel or plastic wrap and put dough to rise in a warm place. Keep out of drafts. Should be doubled in size in 45 minutes to one hour.

Punch down, and let dough rest for 5 or 10 minutes. Turn out onto well floured surface and divide dough into two pieces. Knead and shape into loaf sized shapes and put in well greased or oiled pans. Cover once more with towel and let rise until doubled in size. Bake at 400 degrees for 35 to 40 minutes. Makes 2 large loaves.

For cinnamon rolls, use half the dough, roll out on well floured surface and coat liberally with margarine or butter.

Then coat liberally with brown sugar, cinnamon, raisins, nuts and roll up, sealing edges (Like a jelly roll). Cut into 2 inch wide pieces and put in well greased or oiled pan to rise, covered with towel. When doubled in size, bake at 350 degrees for 20 to 25 minutes. Remove from pan while still hot by inverting pan onto a large plate, so most of the caramel will stay on the rolls. Can be frosted with powdered sugar mixed with butter and a drop or two of milk. Can make dinner rolls or pizza dough with same recipe. Also Fry Bread. Take a small amount of dough, roll out to pancake shape, and fry in butter or margarine until lightly browned on both sides.

MEAT LOAF

One pound or more of ground beef – can use half pork sausage

Salt and pepper

Garlic powder

At least 1 tsp poultry seasoning

1 medium onion, chopped

1 egg

1 pkg or equivalent stuffing mix-(soda crackers, dry oatmeal, stale bread)

1 can tomato sauce OR

1 cup approximately of canned milk

Mix all ingredients well and shape into loaf. Place in greased bread pan or similar pan, put two slices of uncooked bacon on top. Bake in 375 degree oven for 45 minutes or until bacon is cooked. Bake potatoes to go with meat loaf at the same time, starting the potatoes while mixing the meat loaf ingredients. Serve with a vegetable or salad. Use cold leftovers for sandwiches.

MOTHER'S FAMOUS TUNA BUNS

8 long French rolls or 12 round rolls, halved and each half hollowed partially with a spoon, (Reserve the interiors for Bread Pudding or croutons or stuffing)

1 can chunk or minced tuna (6 ½ ounce size)

1 cup grated sharp cheddar cheese

1 medium green pepper, chopped

1 large onion, chopped

1 cup chopped celery

1 small can tomato sauce

Mix all well before filling the halved and hollowed buns.

Bake about 20 minutes at 375 degrees. Check at 15 minutes and if filling is firm, they are done.

These tuna buns make a "meal in a bun". You will find them very tasty and filling. This recipe makes 16 long half buns or 24 smaller half buns and leftovers taste good cold as well as hot.

CORN BREAD OR MUFFINS

1 cup cornmeal

1 cup flour

4 tsps baking powder

¼ cup Splenda or 2 tblsps sugar (or omit sweetener altogether)

1 tsp salt

1 egg

1 cup milk

¼ cup melted butter or oil

Mix dry ingredients together.

Add wet ingredients and stir only until moist (lumps are okay)

Pour into greased 9 x 9 x 2 inch pan or muffin pan, and bake at 425 degrees for 20 to 25 minutes. (15 to 20 minutes for muffins) Makes 12 muffins

ALTERNATE CORNBREAD RECIPE

1 cup cornmeal

1 cup pancake mix

2 tsp baking powder

½ tsp salt

1 egg

1 cup milk

1/8 cup melted butter or oil

BEST OATMEAL COOKIES

1 cup (2 sticks) butter or margarine (yellow Crisco does well)

1 cup firmly packed brown sugar

½ cup granulated sugar

2 eggs

1 tablespoon vanilla

1 ½ cups flour

1 tsp baking soda

1 tablespoon cinnamon

½ tsp salt

3 cups uncooked oats

1 cup raisins

Heat oven to 375 degrees. In large bowl, beat together margarine and sugars until creamy.

Add eggs and vanilla, beat well

Add combined flour, baking soda, cinnamon and salt. Mix well.

Stir in oats and raisins. Drop by rounded tablespoonfuls onto ungreased cookie sheets

Bake 12 to 15 minutes for crisp cookies, 8 to 10 minutes for soft cookies. Cool one minute on cookie sheet; remove to wire rack and cool completely. Yield: 4 dozen

BEST CHOCOLATE CHIP COOKIES

¾ cup butter flavored Crisco (or margarine or butter)

1 ¼ cup brown sugar, packed

1 egg

1 tablespoon vanilla

2 tablespoons milk

1 ½ cups flour

½ teaspoon salt

¾ teaspoon baking soda

Mix first 5 ingredients together until smooth

Mix dry ingredients and add to first mixture, mix until well blended

Add 1 cup chocolate chips and 1 cup walnuts (if desired)

Drop by tablespoonfuls onto ungreased cookie sheet and bake for 10 to 13 minutes in 375 degree oven (10 min. for softer cookies, 13 minutes for crisp)

Note: If nuts are omitted, add another ½ cup chocolate chips

If margarine or butter is used instead of Crisco, omit salt

Variations:

Substitute butterscotch chips and pecans for butter pecan cookies

Substitute white chocolate chips and macadamia nuts for white chocolate/macadamia nut cookies (Yum!) Makes 3 dozen cookies

RICOTTA CHEESE SUGAR COOKIES

1 cup softened butter

2 cups sugar

1 carton full fat ricotta cheese

2 eggs

1 tablespoon vanilla

½ tsp salt

1 tsp baking soda

1 tsp grated lemon zest

4 cups flour

For the Glaze:

1 cup powdered sugar

2-4 tablespoons milk

2 drops almond extract (optional)

Sprinkles

Preheat oven to 350 degrees. Mix cookie ingredients to form a sticky dough. Drop by teaspoonfuls on an ungreased cookie sheet. Bake 10 minutes or until the bottoms turn golden brown (the tops will stay white). Transfer to wire racks to cool. To make glaze, stir milk a few drops at a time, along with the almond extract, if desired, into the powdered sugar in a saucepan. Stir over low heat to create a glaze. Drizzle over cooled cookies and top with colored sprinkles. Makes 3 to 4 dozen cookies

ROLL OUT COOKIES

1 cup butter

1 cup sugar

1 large egg

1 teaspoon vanilla

2 teaspoons baking powder

3 cups flour

In large bowl, cream butter and sugar together. Beat in egg and vanilla. Mix baking powder and flour, add one cup at a time to butter, mixing after each addition. Dough will be stiff. Blend in last flour by hand. If dough gets too stiff, add water a teaspoon at a time. Do not chill.

Divide dough into 2 balls. On floured surface, roll each into circle, 1/8 inch thick for cutouts. Bake at 400 degrees for 5 to 7 minutes until cookies are lightly browned. Decorate as needed, or leave plain. Makes 18 to 24 cookies

SPRITZ COOKIES

1 ½ cups butter

1 cup sugar

1 egg

2 tablespoons milk

1 tsp vanilla

½ tsp almond or rum flavor

3 ½ cups all purpose flour.

1 tsp baking powder

Preheat oven to 375 degrees. Thoroughly cream butter and sugar. Add egg, milk, vanilla and almond extract; beat well. Stir together flour and baking powder, and gradually add to creamed mixture to make smooth dough. Do not chill. Place dough into cookie press and press cookies onto ungreased cookie sheet. Bake 10 to 12 minutes or until lightly brown around edges. Cool on rack

MELTING MOMENTS

1 cup un-sifted flour

½ cup cornstarch

½ cup powdered sugar

¾ cup margarine (or butter flavored Crisco with ½ tsp salt)

1 tsp vanilla

In medium bowl, stir flour, corn starch and powdered sugar. In large bowl with mixer at medium speed, beat margarine until smooth. Add flour mixture and vanilla and beat until combined. Refrigerate one hour. Shape into 1 inch balls. Place about 1 to 1-1/2 inches apart on ungreased cookie sheet; flatten with lightly floured fork. Bake in 375 degree oven 10 to 12 minutes or until edges are lightly browned.
Makes about 3 dozen cookies

VARIATIONS: Rich chocolate: Follow recipe for melting moments. Stir one square semisweet chocolate, melted and cooled into margarine or the equivalent of chocolate chips

Coconut: Add 1 cup finely chopped flaked coconut to flour mixture

Pecan Cinnamon: Add 1/3 cup finely chopped pecans and 1 tsp ground cinnamon to flour mixture

SANTA'S LITTLE WALNUT HELPERS
(Very Good)

TOPPING:

½ cup packed brown sugar

¼ cup sour cream

½ tsp cinnamon

1 cup coarsely chopped walnuts

Prepare topping: In small mixing bowl stir together sugar, sour cream and cinnamon until smooth. Stir in walnuts: Set aside.

DOUGH

½ cup butter or margarine

1 cup packed brown sugar

1 egg

1 tsp vanilla

2 cups flour

½ tsp baking soda

¼ tsp salt

Prepare dough. In mixing bowl, cream butter and sugar. Add egg and vanilla, beat until light and fluffy. On low speed gradually add dry ingredients, beating just until smooth. Divide dough into 12 equal parts. Roll dough into balls and place three inches apart on ungreased baking sheets. With your fingertip, make a wide round depression in the center of each cookie, reaching almost to the edges and leaving a rim. Fill depressions in cookies with walnut topping, mounding fairly high above the rims. Bake in 350 degree oven 15 to 20 minutes, until filling is set. Transfer cookies to rack to cool.

COOKIE ICING:

½ cup powdered sugar

1 tablespoon water.

Mix until smooth.
Drizzle over rims of cookies

NOTE: For smaller cookies, form dough into 24 balls and place two inches apart on baking sheets. Fill and bake as above, reducing baking time to 14 to 15 minutes until filling is set

MOM'S FAMOUS POTATO SALAD

6 Large potatoes, cooked, peeled, cubed

6 hardboiled eggs, sliced up, set aside 1 or 2

5 or 6 celery stalks, washed, chopped up

1 cup mayonnaise

Pickle relish to taste

1 medium onion

Salt and pepper to taste

A few sprinkles of paprika

The night before, or the morning of, cook the potatoes and hard boil the eggs…peel, chop, slice. Put the eggs and potatoes in the fridge to get cold, slice up the celery, set aside.

Use a large mixing bowl, assemble in layers. A layer of cubed potatoes, a layer of celery, a layer of eggs, salt and pepper to taste, a few scoops of mayonnaise and pickle relish, stir it all up and repeat until the bowl is full. Put the whole stirred up salad back in the fridge for at least a couple of hours, overnight is better.

Take the one or two eggs you set aside and slice them into neat little egg shaped pieces…use them to decorate the top of the salad. Sprinkle with paprika. Looks very pretty when you are done and it will be the hit of any get together.

MOM'S STRIP SANDWICHES

2 loaves of bread, 1 white, 1 wheat

1 pkg of good quality bologna, thick sliced *

1 big jar of mayonnaise

1 jar of pickle relish

1 pkg of sliced American cheese **

Each sandwich is 4 slices of bread deep, 2 slices of white and 2 slices of wheat. VERY IMPORTANT to spread the mayonnaise on THIN. This acts as a sort of glue to hold all the pieces together, but too much mayo will only give you a gushy mess.

To assemble:

1st slice of wheat or white, (alternate for color), spread a very thin layer of mayo, place 1 slice of cheese

2nd slice of bread, spread a thin layer of mayo on both sides place on top of the cheese, Put a piece of bologna on the other side of that slice

3rd slice of bread, alternating white and wheat, spread the thin layer of mayo on both sides place one side down on the bologna and a layer of pickle relish on the other side.

4th slice of bread, just put mayo on it and put it on the piece with the pickle relish.

Wrap the sandwich up in tin foil or a zip lock baggy. Put it in the fridge with a not too heavy dinner plate on it overnight. The next morning, use a good bread knife with a serrated edge. Cut off the crusts and put them in a baggy, cut each sandwich into strips about 4 strips each. Serve immediately.

*Use ham, turkey, chicken or what ever kind of lunch meat you like, instead of bologna

**Alternate American and Swiss cheese or use any of the many different spreadable cheeses available. Mom would sometimes use a white cheese with pineapple in it...also very good.

These can be made fresh, but are much harder to slice...don't be afraid to experiment. You can use the crusts you cut off for bread pudding or bread crumbs in meatloaf. Season them, freeze them, make your own croutons.

Glossary

Adze	A hoe-like axe used to chop roots out of the ground
Bench	The flattening of a hillside partway up a mountain
Breakup	When spring comes, snow melts, ice crashes down the rivers and streams, mud everywhere, before things start greening up
Bush	Way out in the country, usually with no road access available
Calving	When large chunks of ice break off of glaciers and fall into the lakes below the glacier
Cheechako	A newcomer or greenhorn
Chinook	A warm wind typically blowing from the south during cold weather. Like the Santa Anna winds in California.
Dog Salmon	Really are chum salmon, but these have fangs and teeth like dogs, therefore nicknamed dog salmon

Gas Car	A small railroad vehicle with rail wheels and an engine which was used by foremen and workers for transportation to work sites along the railroad tracks. Most had canvas sides, metal and glass backs and fronts, and hard wooden or metal seats, like benches inside
Outside	Anywhere NOT in Alaska; also "lower 48" or stateside
Ranger Track Vehicle	A machine with wheels inside of tracks. Has two seats, steered with brakes. Running boards over the tracks on each side where people could sit or fasten objects. Would run over logs and ditches, through water up to two feet deep or so, over rocks and up steep hills. Very versatile and useful machine.
RDC	Rail Diesel Car
Scythe	An old fashioned long curved blade with a long handle for cutting grass, brush and weeds
Slough	(Pronounced slew) a small portion of a river; an area where it becomes a pond or slow-moving stream eventually re-joining the river.
Snow Machine	A vehicle for riding over the snow, with a track and skis – commonly called a snow mobile in other parts of the United States.
States	48 contiguous states separated from Alaska by Canada

Turnaround   What we called our outings on the
              Alaska Railroad during the summers
              when we would catch a train going
              north, ride it to where it met the south
              bound train, get off and board the
              south bound train to get back home
              again

Whiteout   When the air is filled with falling or
              blowing snow and/or fog and visibility
              is zero

***

Pictures

The photographs scattered throughout this book, and in the previous book Journey to a Dream, are from many sources and span almost fifty years. The early years pictures were mostly taken on little flash cube film cameras by prolific amateurs. Many times we had to crop out a finger or strap inadvertently left over the lens while shooting. Over and under exposed shots as well as shots taken with flash when no flash should have been used all add to the complexity of getting pictures in the book that come close to acceptable.

Many of the early pictures are faded, bent, water stained, fingerprinted, taped or other interesting modifications. My son Bud spent many hours working with the photographs in this book to get them so they could be printed here large enough to show what the subject is without being totally washed out or so dark as to occlude the subject.

Most of the pictures in these books were indeed taken by the Lovel family, and where it is known who specifically took the picture, credit is given. Some Pictures came from outside the family from friends, and on each of those proper credit is given. If we missed giving proper credit on any of the photographs, we extend our sincere apologies, and will make note if it in our next book (Lord Willing!).

This section is of pictures that did not specifically fit into the story, but help show the richness of our lives at our wonderful homestead. They are in no particular order or grouping. I hope you enjoy them as much as we do!

If you wish to see all the pictures in this book and Journey to a Dream in the original color and/or size, please visit our web site at:
http://shermanpublishing.webs.com/

Clyde and my THIRTEEN grandchildren. Back row, left to right: Kate Bryner, Nathan Lovel, Jackie Lovel, Rachel Finley, Christa Finley, Michael Finley, Timmy Finley. Front row, left to right: Greg Finley, Vanessa Lovel, Amanda Lovel, Danny Finley, Mary-Alice Lanni, Rhys Bryner.

*Alaska Railroad Train Engineer and life long family friend Gordon Larson.
Gordon is the son of the Gold Creed Section Foreman Harold Larson and was for
many years one of our nearest neighbors, only five miles away.
Photo by Richard Long*

*Granddaughters Amanda and Vanessa playing in a pool we keep filled during dry
spells during the summers, just in case of wild fires. Lightening and trains set fires
during the dry season, and we are our own fire department.*

Black Bears; the one above is shooing her cubs up a tree in our back yard. The one below is walking on the top of the rail in front of a slow moving train, completely ignoring the train! The homestead is just around the bend at the top of the picture. Photo below taken by Richard Long

Cranberry Picking is a much appreciated chore in the fall. Debbie, Mary and Lisa picking berries near the house in 1972. A more recent photograph of cranberries, fall 2009 by Bud Lovel

June, 1967. Bud using our first piece of machinery for plowing the ground; a sears roto-tiller. It was woefully inadequate for the task of breaking new ground but was all we could afford at the time. In this picture Bud is tilling the garden after the previous years harvest.

Spring, 1965. <u>Good Clean Dirt!</u> The family that gets dirty together... We worked and played hard during the years at the homestead. "Improving" the land to qualify for ownership of the homestead required years of long hard hours of brutal physical labor.

Cabbages and chickweed. The summer of 1972 was good for the garden. Coleslaw and sauerkraut in abundance from rock hard heads weighing up to forty pounds, each!

Summer 1965. Bud with his prize Cabbage.

On left, Clyde and his mother, Ethel, at Montana Creek in 1967. On right, Clyde in 1970, standing near the cabin site above the homestead in the Talkeetna Mountains.

Clyde heading down to the tracks to catch the train to town.

147

Caribou crossing the highway near Glennallen.

Clyde Winter '09 standing on the ground after shoveling away eight feet of snow pack to get to the outhouse.

Building the second story to provide bedrooms for the four kids and eliminate the leaky flat tarpaper roof!

1967. Clyde with our first snowmachine; a 1966 Polaris Mustang with a 15 inch wide track with steel cleats and a single cylinder 15 horse two cycle engine.

Young Bald Eagle, just about finished getting it's adult feathers.

Young Bull Moose Near Bud's Home in Wasilla.

Cow moose in Bud's backyard in Wasilla. She has two calves not in the picture.

Young cow moose near Bud's home in Wasilla. Her calf is hidden in the woods behind her. All photos on this page by Bud Lovel

Shelley, Bud, Lisa and Debbie posed for a picture at Cynthia and Bud's wedding. 1997

Shelley, Bud, Lisa and Debbie from four different pictures from a summer 32 years earlier: 1965. Bud used Photoshop to blend the pictures together; the one of Lisa had only half her face showing.

Family time on the train. Long time family friend, Steve Culver is the Conductor. From left to right: Steve Culver, Amanda wearing Steve's hat, Behind her, Nathan clowning around, Clyde seated, and directly in front of Clyde you can see Vanessa's head and nose. Behind Clyde, Jackie, and next to Clyde, Mary, also seated.

Another shot with Vanessa wearing Steve's hat.

Lovel family 1972. Left to right: Debbie, Bud, Clyde, Mary, Shelley, and Lisa. Probably celebrating Mary and Clyde's Birthdays and anniversary.

The Lovel family after Shelley left for the convent, 1973. From left to right: back row; Bud, Clyde, Mary. Front row; Debbie, and Lisa.

About midway between Talkeetna and Sherman a pair of swans raises a family every year. Here, an adult and two chicks swim away as the train passes. Photo by Richard Long.

Winter 1968. Looking from the tracks just south of the homestead. The little dark line with the snow on top of it is our little home in the vast wilderness. Sometimes it really sank in how remote our home was.

Passengers and small freight were delivered by the RDC during the summer and regular passenger trains in the winter. Here Clyde (facing) and Tim Finley (taking box from door) are unloading groceries after a trip to town to stock up.

Heavy freight like building supplies, lumber, fuel, and machinery are brought by a large truck on rail wheels, called the Tundra. Here we are getting lumber and roofing for one of the many ongoing maintenance or upgrade projects to keep our home warm and dry.

Mary shot a Lynx that was about to attack our dog Johnny. 1967

Mary and her garden flowers. 1972

Mary's mother Rachel Zirwes and Shelley at the convent. 1976

Above – Rachel Finley contemplating and giving her self a good talking to about higher education. Below – Graduating! We are all proud of you Rachel.